A

Queen's

CROWN

A Sacred Blueprint to Awaken Your
Calling, Embody Inner Excellence, Reign in
Royal Authority, and Create a Legacy

A

Queen's

CROWN

Dr. Lougenia J. Rucker

Unless otherwise noted, all scriptures are from the Holy Bible (NKJV)

Published by: Divine Diamonds Ministries |
Dr. Lougenia J. Rucker, Philadelphia, PA

Graphic/Interior Design: Virtual Way Professional Services

To contact the Author: Dr. Lougenia J. Rucker

484-443-3889

Email: DrLougenia@trailblazingtransformations.com

Printed in the United States of America

Disclaimer: The information in this book is not meant to replace the advice of certified financial or legal professionals. Please consult a licensed advisor in matters of your financial legacy and well-being.

Dedication

I dedicate *A Queen's Crown* to all the beautiful, brilliant Queens who carry the courage to serve and love.

To my Daughter/Neice, Shay La'rren, God-Daughters, Spiritual Daughters, God-Sisters, Sisters-n-Love, and Nieces, may you always know who you are, walk boldly in your brilliance, and never let the weight of the crown stop you from wearing it with grace and love. You were born to reign.

And in loving memory of the first Queen I ever knew....
My Beloved Mother, Sara B. Johnson. Your unwavering love, daily prayers, and legacy of strength are forever imprinted on my heart. Thank you for rubbing oil on my feet when I couldn't stand, and for imparting into my spirit long before I knew my calling. I rise because you kneeled. I lead because you served. I reign because you believed.

This crown is as much yours as it is mine.

Contents

Foreword by Dr. Pam Perry

Founder, PamPerryPR.com | Publisher, Speakers Magazine

Purpose isn't something we find—it's something we remember. And Dr. Lougenia J. Rucker has not only remembered her own purpose, but she has made it her mission to help other women do the same—boldly, audaciously, and with divine authority.

In my over two decades of working with powerhouse women, legacy builders, and thought leaders who are shifting culture, I've learned to spot a woman who doesn't just *talk* impact—she *walks* it. Dr. Lougenia is that woman. Every word she speaks, every platform she graces, and every life she touches carries a divine assignment. And with *A Queen's Crown*, she has given us more than a book. She's given us a blueprint. A movement. A sacred mandate to rise.

This isn't just ink on paper, it's oil for your crown.

Dr. Lougenia has poured into this work from a deep well of wisdom, experience, and spiritual revelation. What you'll find in these pages is not fluff or feel-good phrases. You'll find sacred strategies. Real talk. Holy reminders of who you are, whose you are, and what you were *truly* born to do. She breaks down the crushing seasons without sugar-coating them, while simultaneously lifting women into their coronation moment—fully healed, wholly seen, and spiritually equipped.

She writes like she lives—with clarity, conviction, and courage. Whether you've known her as a keynote speaker, coach, mentor, or minister, you already know this: Lougenia doesn't hold back. She doesn't shrink. And she refuses to let *you* do it either.

This book is drenched in divine assignment. It's not just meant to be read—it's meant to be *activated*.

I'm honored to pen the foreword of *A Queen's Crown*, not only because I believe in Dr. Lougenia's mantle, but because I believe in the women this book is called to reach. Women who are done dimming their light. Women are ready to rise in leadership and build with a legacy in mind. Women like you—yes, *you*—who know you were created for *more*.

So if you've ever questioned your calling, wrestled with your worth, or wondered if your pain had purpose—this book is your confirmation. If you've been carrying vision but lacked a roadmap, Dr. Lougenia is handing you the scroll. And if you've been praying for a sign to stop playing small and finally step into your queenly authority?

You're holding it.

A Queen's Crown is more than a read—it's a royal recalibration. Let it anoint you, challenge you, and ultimately, crown you. Because your time is now. And queens don't wait—they reign.

With love, power, and PR,
Dr. Pam Perry
www.PamPerryPR.com
Publisher, *Speakers Magazine*
Host, *Get Out There and Get Known Podcast*

Preface

A Divine Disruption

What began as a response to a few interview questions for an exclusive media feature quickly became a spiritual catalyst. As I began to articulate my journey, unexpected downloads from heaven started pouring in, awaking a deeper message, a divine mandate, and ultimately, a new movement. I suddenly realized that this was *not* just another season. This was my Crowning Year, a divine gateway into new dimensions of excellence, purpose, power, and prophetic legacy.

After celebrating the 8th year of my *Game-Changer Program's Ultimate Gala*, I found myself standing at a spiritual crossroads. Everything was beautiful, and the decorative ballroom and Gala will go down in history as one of the best creative ventures. However, what had once been so fulfilling was now met with a divine unrest. I was truthfully tired and burned out. A bit challenged because I knew deep in my spirit that God was requiring something *different* from me. Something deeper. Something more sacred. And it wasn't just about reinvention, it was about realignment.

This book was birthed through that moment of divine disruption.

It was in this place of internal recalibration that the Lord began whispering truths to me about my crown, and what it really meant to carry oil, to wear royal identity with integrity, and to rise from the ashes of past seasons *not as a victim, but as an anointed vessel.*

There have been so many defining moments in my life, each one carrying its own crushing and its own anointing. From surviving a horrific early childhood hit-and-run that could have stolen my destiny, the unfortunate clash and legal ending of my brief marriage that caused a great loss of confidence and personal self-esteem, to shifting from an abandoned, divorced caregiver for my beloved mother, into an award-winning, anointed marketplace ministry leader. From climbing the corporate ladder in healthcare management to suddenly becoming a heart failure survivor, gasping for breath, and finding a new purpose in pain, fear, and loneliness.

Every twist. Every test. Every tear. They were all a part of my crowning journey of inner strength, inner excellence, and ultimately inner peace and prosperity.

This book is not just a reflection, it's a sacred blueprint. A prophetic guide for women who are ready to heal, rise, serve, reign, and leave a generational legacy. It's for the woman who has poured out until she's empty... the one who has been overlooked, misjudged, or mishandled. The woman who's been hiding behind titles and accomplishments while secretly struggling to believe in her own royal worth.

And if that woman is *you*, then let this be your clarion call.

A Queen's CROWN is the oil-soaked journey of adjusting what life tried to tilt, redeeming what was nearly lost, and discovering the holy beauty of becoming the woman you were born to be.

You are not defined by what broke you. You are crowned by what you *rose from*. I am so grateful that God can turn ashes into beauty.

This book carries no shame—only oil, only glory, only testimony.

So now, my beloved sister...take a deep breath. Exhale the guilt, the fear, the hiding, and prepare to walk with me, chapter by chapter, into your crowning moment.

In His service with love and divine honor,
Dr. Lougenia J. Rucker
Apostle of Excellence. Vessel of Oil. Iconic Queen.

Introduction

Crowning Year

The Sacred Call and Blueprint to Inner Excellence, Royal Authority, and Generational Legacy

This is your divine transformational **Crowning Year**, and this book is a masterpiece unveiling a sacred moment in time. It is a bold clarion call – A Royal Invitation - to rise into your next dimension of higher purpose, kingdom power, and profound prophetic impact.

You are not here by accident. Every trial, every tear, and every triumph has led you to this Kairos time of a divine alignment where Heaven and Earth converge to propel you into your ordained destiny.

Every chapter has been intentionally written to guide you through the unveiling of your divine identity, your royal authority, and the embodiment of inner peace, excellence, and brilliance of an abundant mindset and prosperous lifestyle. This positions you to reign on purpose and in authority, experience fulfillment, and build a lasting legacy for generations.

Queens have been anointed, set apart, and positioned for leadership throughout history. Their crowns were not merely ornamental; they symbolized regal authority, wisdom, power, leadership, and legacy. Symbolically, we are using the crown as a key image featured throughout the book's *Coronation Journey* of personal growth and development, including identity, healing, consecration, and transformation.

I am so grateful for the spiritual download of a divine Method of Empowerment and a prophetic acronym for C.R.O.W.N. We will discuss this powerful framework in more detail in Chapter Five, and how it will enable you to walk boldly in your renewed identity and seal the Future Queen in your heart.

During this time of yielding and refining, your anointing oil of empowerment will flow, your mantle of purpose secured, and your kingdom assignment activated. This book is a sacred blueprint that will walk you through the prophetic chambers of transformational encounters needed to step fully into your crowned assignments. The crown isn't just for ceremonial purposes or beautification. But for battle-tested queens who carry weight and wisdom.

The journey to the Crowning of any Queen is never without its crushing and clarifying elements. I shared my personal story of what was intended to have a tragic ending, but by great faith and perseverance, it was turned into a trailblazing path of purpose and power.

Diamonds are forged under pressure, and gold is purified by fire. You have been through the refining fires of life, emerging stronger, wiser, and more radiant. Now it is time to reign with purpose, authority, and power.

The Divine Flow Structure of the Book....

This transformational book is infused with the prophetic anointing that is upon my life and layered with unfiltered creativity to awaken, unbox, unlock, and unleash your next-level purpose and power. I am anointed to create, and it is my superpower. I firmly believe that your soul prosperity is always connected to your deeper purpose; therefore, generational wealth is also attached to it.

Here is the overall structure of the three major sections of this transformational book:

- Teaching, Empowerment Tools, Activations, and Revelations
- Scripture References and Meditations
- Prayers, Decrees, and Declarations
- Personal Stories, Royal Reflections, and Deep Dive Questions
- Journal Note Pages and Exercises
- Bonuses and Free Gifts.

You can think of this book as a Reigning and Training Manual and a queenly Blueprint teaching principles and spiritual laws needed to transform your thoughts, behavior, and perspectives, which are necessary for personal fulfillment and destiny. This journey is not a casual read, but a royal purification process of preparation and elevation. The oil dripping from each page has a sweet fragrance and a divine weight of the anointing.

"Destiny is not a matter of chance, it is a matter of choice," - William Jennings Bryan

As you turn these pages, you will be guided through a revelatory process that will ignite your faith, sharpen your clarity, and establish you in dominion. Align your heart with the wisdom revealed on the pages and dive deep into the reflections and activating questions. This is not just a book—it is a prophetic portal, unlocking new realms of wisdom, wealth, and unwavering confidence in who God has called you to be.

Prepare to be wrapped in a royal mantle of inner excellence, consecrated with a fresh anointing, released to move forward with divine acceleration and radical authority. In addition:

- **Align with your royal identity:** recognize and embrace yourself as a Kingdom Queen, set apart for a powerful purpose.
- **Receive fresh oil**: be anointed anew for the next dimension of your assignment with new realms of revelation unlocked.
- **Embrace your spiritual authority:** walk unapologetically in the dominion and influence God has given you.
- **Build and sustain generational wealth:** position yourself for generational impact and greater provisions.
- **Step into your prophetic reign:** position and move with precision, knowing that the future is within you, and every step is ordained and backed by Heaven.

Prayers have been sent up, unlocking realms for women to walk boldly in their royal identity. The atmosphere is set with the fragrance of the Future. Heaven is leaning in to meet you right where you are. Listen, take your time as you experience Heaven's Sacred Spa encounters because it will clothe you in majesty and His anointing. Do the inner work at the end of each chapter to unlock your purpose and uncover your brilliance.

This sacred journey is not merely about external success or titles; it is about cultivating the inner brilliance that prepares you to reign with boldness, wisdom, and grace. As you turn these pages, you will awaken deeper levels of faith, unlock your calling, strengthen your spiritual identity, and build a generational legacy rooted in truth, excellence, and enduring wealth.

This is your Crowning Year, the year where you break barriers, shatter limitations and limiting thoughts, and walk fully in your inner excellence of strength and beauty. The heavens are open, the oil is flowing, your CROWN awaits, and your generational legacy begins now.

Are you ready to respond to your Sacred Call?

The King is waiting...

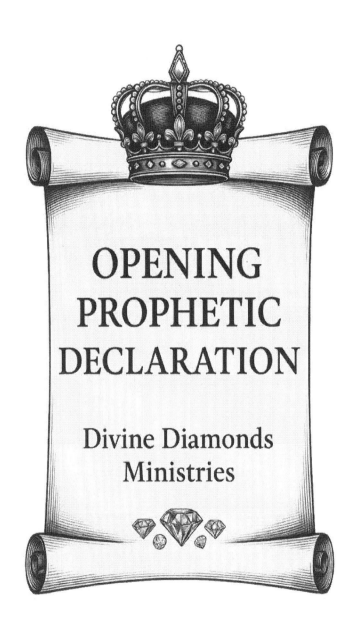

OPENING PROPHETIC DECLARATION

Divine Diamonds
Ministries

Opening Prophetic Declaration

ROYAL ONE, your time has come. Heaven has summoned you to the inner chambers for a divine coronation. You are standing under an open heaven— on holy ground—where oil is flowing, mantles are being released, and crowns are descending.

This is your Crowning Year—your Kairos moment of becoming. You have been refined by fire, preserved by grace, and called forth to reign in excellence and brilliance.

Every crushing, every silent moment of fear, every hidden tear has produced an oil so fragrant it announces your arrival before you speak a word.

You are not broken; you are becoming. You are not forgotten; you are being formed. You are not behind; you are being prepared.

I decree that you are rising with clarity, confidence, courage, and excellence. Your inner well-being is being strengthened. Your calling is being confirmed. Your concerns are being answered by divine surrender and alignment. Your purpose is being redefined on higher grounds. Your territory, influence, and impact are being expanded.

This is the hour of clarification, activation, and multiplication. You are anointed to speak, birth, build, shine, and blaze a life and legacy of fulfillment. No more doubting or second-guessing. No more shrinking or playing small. No more dimming your light. Heaven has anointed you to release and authorized you to reign.

Live on purpose. Walk in excellence without guilt. Wear your crown boldly. Love fiercely. Lead prophetically. Release the oil of your assignment into the earth.

This is not just your moment. This is your movement. And it begins… NOW.

Divine Diamonds Ministries Collective

PART ONE

ASHES to BEAUTY –

The Inner Work and Healing Encounter

"He gives beauty for ashes, the oil of joy for mourning, the garment of praise for the spirit of heaviness…"

– Isaiah 61:3

CHAPTER 1

Crowning Act of a Queen

"Before I formed you in the womb, I knew you [and approved of you as My chosen instrument], And before you were born, I consecrated you [to Myself as My own]; I have appointed you as a prophet to the nations."

- Jeremiah 1:5 (AMP)

Enter Heaven's Sacred Spa of Consecration

This is your personal and royal invitation to prepare your heart to step into Heaven's Sacred Spa of Consecration and Anointing, a transformational journey, a sacred consecration and a divine immersion where your soul will be revived, renewed and soaked in the oil of the anointing, your heart healed by truth and love, and your spirit baptized in clarity, insights and revelation.

Self-care and self-love practices are more than sleep, massages, manicures, and pedicures; they also include making hard decisions, facing significant turning points in your life, while at the same time, making time to love and comfort yourself. This is your Kairos time and a sacred season of preparation for what I will call the "coronation" process of transformation and elevation.

Enter these sacred chambers of each chapter with great expectation and excitement. Seek and expect a transformational encounter as you experience the power of anointing and a holistic and spiritual release in the realm of the spirit.

You are being summoned to a spiritual encounter and coronation for the act of crowning you as a Kingdom Queen. Over the next few chapters, prepare your heart for a spiritual encounter that can shift the very trajectory of your life. Divine portals will begin to open up and show you revelations and insights into your new season, for God has placed the future in your heart. (Ecclesiastes 3:11)

God desires to have a personal relationship with you and partner with you to co-create the future he has planned for your life. Through the power of prayer, you can bring heaven to earth. You can call those things that are not as though they are. Give yourself permission to partner with God to birth these things into the earth realm.

As you move forward, walk by faith and obey God and follow his instructions through the revelations and hidden truths revealed by the Holy Spirit. When you obey, God will do that which is above and beyond your ability, the supernatural. Increase your faith by hearing, reading, meditating, and decreeing the Word. Fully surrender and submit your life, desires, and plans to the Lord. This will allow God to flow fully through you without hindrance.

Heaven does not crown without first consecration

Every woman desiring to be crowned as a Queen of Faith must first be willing and allow herself to surrender to God and allow the fleshly garments of her past season to be removed so that she can be adorned with new and purified garments of praise, worship, and authority.

This process is not an external or cosmetic experience. But an internal encounter of detoxification, purification, and consecration. Heaven's Sacred Spa serves as a transitional space for the re-identification, re-alignment, and re-direction of your life, preparing you for elevation, leadership, manifestation, and domination.

You will not only be crowned so that your brilliance will shine for all to see, but you are crowned to serve and to reign. True power, success, and wealth lie within giving of yourself.

The Coronation and the Call to your Throne

[17] The king loved Esther more than all the *other women*, and she obtained grace and favor in his sight more than all the virgins; so he set the royal crown upon her head and made her queen instead of Vashti. [18] Then the king made a great feast, the Feast of Esther, for all his officials and servants; and he proclaimed a holiday in the provinces and gave gifts according to the generosity of a King. – Esther 2:17-18

In the scripture, you find the official coronation of Esther – first the separation, consecration, and the anointing process of the Queen to be. After her time of purification, she was privately taken to the King. Next, the adoration and love of the king. Then came the crowning of his queen and the public celebration.

The act of crowning is a royal, sacred ceremony of identifying the queen, placing the crown upon the queen, signifying and amplifying her authority and power. For the sake of this book and purpose, we will also include being anointed with holy oil as part of the sacred ritual, spiritual impartation, and affirmation.

In the spirit realm, your identification, coronation, and destination were ordained before you were formed in your mother's womb according to Jeremiah 1:5. Heaven has decreed you chosen, set apart, and anointed to reign. Now is your set time to shift into your queenly mindset, lifestyle, and step into the earthly manifestation of Heaven's decree and appointment of time.

You were born for this. The crowning is the heavenly seal upon your life and your royal Kingdom identity. Before Queen Esther could walk boldly into her royal assignment of service, she first surrendered to a season of preparation. Her mind, body, and soul were renewed, refined, anointed, and repositioned in the secret place of the private chambers of the palace before she ever stood in her public role, responsibilities, and authority. (Esther 2:12).

This is your personal "Esther" moment, your time to shift and arise out of the ashes of hurt, pain, scarcity, unworthiness, unforgiveness, imposter syndrome, broken promises, betrayal, abandonment, rejection, dissatisfaction, discomfort, and fear created by your current lifestyle.

This is your time to anoint yourself, cultivate unwavering belief in yourself, and your mindset of abundance and prosperity. Prepare to enter into the beauty of transformation. Your *Heaven's Spa of the Spirit* is a dedicated space where you can visualize and emotionalize the release of old garments for the exchange of a royal robe, a new beginning, and where your fresh, creative oil can flow.

What Your Kingdom Crown Represents

Your Crown is a prophetic announcement of the arrival of your new signature lifestyle and brand. It is a divine declaration, speaking boldly in the spirit realm to the following:

- **Your Royal Identity** — Daughter of the King, fearfully and wonderfully made with inner resilience, excellence, and beauty.
- **Your Spiritual Authority** — Assigned and authorized to decree, declare, and dismantle.
- **Your Legacy and Lineage** — Anointed Vessel and carrier of generational oil, unlocking wealth, wisdom, and wonders.
- **Your Mandate and Mantle** — Commissioned to build, birth, bless, serve, and create generational legacies.

This is your set time to:

- **Renew your mindset and refresh your spirit** for self-mastery, identification, and alignment with your Calling. Read and meditate on the scriptures and recommended readings for healing, elevation, revelation, and transformation.

- **Remove the mental blocks and release the residue** of past seasons that tried to delay, deny, hinder, block your blessings, and strip your crown. Ask for forgiveness and forgive others. Get out of your own way and allow yourself to be healed and made whole.

- **Receive, soak in, and embrace the oil** of the anointing that calms your mind, soothes and restores your soul, and prepares you to reign with wisdom, grace, authority, and excellence.

Entering the Prophetic Coronation Chambers

The Holy Spirit is summoning you to your sacred **Prophetic Coronation Chamber**: a private, set-apart, personalized place for release, healing, and a divine encounter to:

- Meet one-on-one with the King, your Creator.
- Realign yourself to your original intended state of wholeness, peace with the release of every limiting belief, burden, insecurity, anxiety, and fear.
- Reposition yourself with the anointing of fresh oil to reframe your words as you *reimagined* a NEW place of wholeness and wealth.

This is not a microwave process. You cannot rush the inner healing and renewal process. Your Creator holds time in His hands. As you patiently surrender, the divine portals of Change open. This is where mantles descend, instructions are released, excellence is elevated, and your spiritual authority is activated.

This chamber becomes your **realm of rest, quietness, and surrender to just Being**. Knowing you, forgiving you, liking you, and accepting you. Silence the noise, quiet the chaos, and lean into the stillness where Heaven speaks.

Yes God still speaks today.

God speaks through many and various ways. Here are some key forms that God speaks through:

1. Through His Word (scriptures). 2 Timothy 3:16-17
2. In an audible voice. Hebrews 4:7
3. In an impression on the heart. 2 Samuel 5:12
4. Through people.1 Corinthians 12:1
5. With signs. Luke 21:25
6. With visions. Acts 2:17
7. With dreams. Job 33:14

How to activate your ability to hear from God:

- Dedicate time to praise and worship Him.
- Pray and ask the Lord what's in His heart concerning you.

- After praying and worshipping God, sit still and listen quietly.
- Read the scriptures.
- Use a notebook or journal to capture the words of God.
- Take a journal or notebook and begin to write down what you hear, believe, and perceive that God is saying to you.
- Ask yourself if what you heard agrees with the scriptures. God will never speak contrary to His written Word.

Wisdom Crowning Keys:

- Every queen must **bow before she is crowned**.
- Heaven crowns those who have surrendered and **bowed in obedience.**
- Your surrendered posture becomes your **crowning key**.
- This is not about **performance**; it is about **positioning your heart**.
- Heaven is watching not for perfection, but for **posture**.

Royal Reflections and Prophetic Activations

Unveil the Queen Within: A Time of Sacred Reflection, Clarity, and Courageous Alignment

Create your dedicated time of consecration. As you emerge from your personal Sacred Spa of Consecration, take time to pause, reflect, and respond from the depths of your heart. The following guided reflections are designed to help you get still, gain clarity, realign your mindset, reframe your words, reclaim your confidence, and courageously position yourself for crowning and thriving.

Mental Reset

- How am I nurturing my spiritual crown through daily communion with God, and what new sacred practices can elevate my inner excellence?
- What beliefs or behaviors have tried to limit your ability to see yourself as prospering royalty in God's Kingdom?

- How can you honor your physical temple to sustain the strength, stamina, and excellence required for my royal assignment?
- In what areas of your life do you sense God is inviting you to shift from survival to significance?
- **Clarity in Calling**

  3. What vision or divine assignment has God placed on your heart that must now come to the forefront?

  4. What distractions or distortions need to be removed or released so you can clearly see the next step?
- **Confidence Booster**

  5. Where have you lost confidence in your ability to lead, serve, or impact others, and what truth from God's Word can you declare to reverse that lie?

  6. Recall a past victory that reminds you of your strength and divine anointing. How can you use that testimony as fuel for this season?

- **Courage to Rise**

  7. What fears or insecurities must be laid down before stepping fully into your coronation moment?

  8. What bold, obedient action will you take this week to walk toward your divine crowning?

Sacred Consecration Action Steps:

Find a quiet comfortable place to sit with the Holy Spirit. Light a candle, worship God, open your heart to him, invite and welcome the Holy Spirit to commune with you.

In your journal, write a *Royal Decree of Identity* — a powerful affirmation of who you are as a crowned daughter of the King. Begin with:

"I Am a Queen who has been crowned by Heaven. I choose to rise out of the ashes of _____. I now walk in the fullness of my identity as a vessel of _____."

Declare this daily for the next *7 days* and expect a divine shift in your mindset.

Scripture Meditation & Soaking Declarations

Sit at the Feet of the King. Soak in the Word. Be Washed by Truth.

As you close this sacred chapter, take intentional time to meditate on these anointed scriptures. Allow them to speak to your spirit, soften your heart, and saturate your soul in divine truth. Read them slowly. Declare them boldly. Listen for Heaven's whisper.

Jeremiah 1:5 (AMP)
"Before I formed you in the womb, I knew you [and approved of you as My chosen instrument], and before you were born I consecrated you [to Myself as My own]; I have appointed you as a prophet to the nations."

Soaking Declaration:
I was known before I was born. I am chosen. I am consecrated. I am appointed for such a time as this.

Esther 2:17
"The king loved Esther more than all the other women,

and she obtained grace and favor in his sight... so he set the royal crown upon her head and made her queen..."

Soaking Declaration:

I walk in uncommon favor. Heaven has placed the royal crown upon my head. I accept the call to reign with grace, wisdom, and purpose.

Ecclesiastes 3:11 (NIV)

"He has made everything beautiful in its time. He has also set eternity in the human heart..."

Soaking Declaration:

My time is now. I release what it was. I receive what shall be. I am aligned with Heaven's perfect timing. My life is a reflection of His eternal beauty.

Optional Soaking Practice:

Create a still moment in worship — turn on soft instrumental soaking music, close your eyes, and breathe deeply. Read these scriptures aloud. Then simply *listen*. Journal any words, impressions, or visions the Holy Spirit reveals to you.

Meditation Scripture

Isaiah 43:19

[19] Behold, I will do a new thing, now it shall spring forth; Shall you not know it? I will even make a road in the wilderness and rivers in the desert.

NOTE PAGE
Crowning Insights and Revelations

CHAPTER 2

The Crowning Oil Unlock: When Heaven Pours and Identity is Sealed

"It is like the precious oil upon the head, running down on the beard, the beard of Aaron, running down on the edge of his garments..."   - Psalm 133:2

There is a moment in every Queen's *becoming* where the Heavens pause and pour upon her.

Where the whispers of Angels echo through eternity and the holy oil is released not by man, but by the very hand of God.

This moment is not loud. It is not hurried. It is holy. It is the Crowning Oil Unlock.

A divine and irreversible internal shift where your royal identity is revealed, sealed, and destiny is confirmed.

This is not a surface touch but a saturating anointing where the oil is released and poured out upon you. This outpouring encounter is not for pampering but for preparation and purification. An encounter that doesn't just visit you, but marks you, changes you, and prepares you for Kingdom service and dominion.

You're not being introduced to the crown, but you're being immersed in the anointing oil process that makes the crown yours. The oil cleanses your wounds, mends the broken, refreshes your soul, and marks you as set apart for His purposes.

The immersion in the anointing oil carries your testimony. My personal story of corporate manager to primary caregiver is living proof that the oil flows from the crushing. I was involuntarily released from my corporate management job with a miraculous well-paid executive 2-year severance package (including paid benefits, holidays and medical coverage), which allowed me to assume the full-time job of caring for my disabled mother until her very last breath. But God allowed the crushing of my professional career to unlock a deeper anointing, richer life, and the birth of Divine Diamonds Ministries.

The oil of healing, restoration, wisdom, authority, and transformation didn't come from comfort, it came from collision. What the enemy of my soul meant to destroy me only pressed me deeper into a personal relationship with Him and divine purpose. Every Queen will have her own crushing story, but your crushing is not your conclusion. It is the gateway to divine identity, fresh oil, and the powerful anointing.

What is the Crowning Oil Unlock?

The *Crowning Oil Unlock* is the divine moment when Heaven publicly acknowledges what was privately formed. It is the activation point where God reveals to you, and even to the world, that the shaking, crushing, and refinement season was not in vain, but for your good and His Glory.

This oil isn't cosmetic or fragrance. It represents a precious connection and a Kingdom covenant. It symbolizes purpose, healing, supernatural empowerment, assignments, authority, and power. The Wise Virgins understood this (Matthew 25 1-13) and they preserved and protected their expensive oil.

Likewise, you must guard your oil and protect it at all costs. The Oil represents the Crown and:

- **Healing Balm:** It anoints the broken places, soothes and empowers your soul after a season of disruptions and spiritual warfare.

- **Clarity of purpose:** The oil illuminates your vision and opens your spiritual ears to hear what God is saying. It empowers you to do what God is calling you to do.

- **Divine Authorization:** When you anoint yourself, you agree with Heaven's decree over your life. You allow God to lead you, direct you, and order your steps.

- **Empowerment to Build:** Fresh oil is your spiritual weapon and the fuel you need to birth, build, and bless without burnout and shipwreck

The oil of the crown doesn't just rest upon your head, but it breaks yokes, imparts wisdom, heals wounds, and commissions you with sacred authority.

The Oil knows who you are becoming, even before you do.

- It flows and heals where your obedience and trust reside.
- It finds dark and hidden places for illumination and transformation.
- It unlocks the chambers of your soul that religion, rejection, and ridicule tried to deny and shut down.

The Crowning Oil Comes with a Sound

Every unlocking has a sound. The oil speaks before the crown appears. Can you hear it?

- *It sounds like surrender.*
- *It sounds like healing tears.*
- *It sounds like alignment.*
- *It sounds like "yes, Lord, even though it hurts."*
- *It sounds like the whispers of angels and the hush of heaven.*

The oil comes not just to anoint you, but to affirm that your preparation has met its appointed moment.

When you anoint your head, your hands, your heart, and even your feet, you are declaring:

- My heart is mended, healed, and guarded from betrayals and heartbreaks.
- My mind is renewed and set apart for divine wisdom and strategy.
- My hands are anointed to build wealth and create generational legacies.
- My feet are guided into the right rooms, assignments, and territories.

Heaven's sacred spa is a place for self-love and self-care to be infused with His unconditional love, peace, dominion, authority, and the sound of abundance.

The Sacred Spiritual Prophetic Chambers Activation Process: Anoint Yourself with The Oil -

1. *Daughter, get in a comfortable, sweet spot and gently close your eyes.*
2. *Breathe deeply and relax.*
3. *Say a heartfelt prayer of surrender, release, and invite the Holy Spirit to commune with you.*
4. *Recognize His presence and allow yourself to be comfortable in His presence.*
5. *Take a little amount of the oil and anoint your forehead.*
6. *Pray, speak, and decree life and healing over your life as you anoint yourself. (If you prefer, you can anoint additional members of your body as well)*
7. *Imagine the Oil of Heaven pouring over your head and down to your feet.*

8. *Experience the empowering, pure, warm, and flowing fragrance of His anointing.*

9. *Sit quietly in the moment, feel and embrace the presence of the Holy Spirit.*

10. *Yield to His presence and allow Him to speak, heal, and set you free. Surrender and feel the consecration and intentional flow of His power (over fear, trauma, loss, rejection, wounds, and unhealed places).*

11. *Cry if need be.*

12. *Shout if need be.*

13. *Forgive yourself and others.*

14. *Whatever you do, be sure to let go and release all of the old to prepare for the new.*

15. *Listen and allow the Lord to speak if he so desires.*

16. *Now, slowly open your eyes.*

17. *Know that you are loved and healed.*

18. *Give Him a thank you, praise, and worship Him.*

19. *Take Holy Communion. (I Corinthians 11:23-26)*

20. *Journal to preserve your prophetic whispers.*

21. *GLORY TO GOD.*

Repeat this activating and anointing process daily or as often as you prefer. Be sure to record any "words" that you believe that you heard the Lord speak to you.

You are being activated and unlocked not just for a purpose, but for presence and glory. His fragrance is not for fame; it is your scent in the spirit realm that marks you as royalty, announcing your arrival before you even speak.

In the quietness and stillness of the Prophetic Chambers, allow the oil to flow. When you sit, rest, and wait in His presence, as the Heavens open over you. This is the divine and sacred spa, the inner sanctuary where oil is poured out, not rushed for the sake of consecration and transformation.

As you unlock the Oil:

- You are becoming His temple that carries the oil.
- You are becoming the answer to a generation's cry.

- You are being crowned and consecrated for such a time as this.

Feed your faith daily by meditating on the Word of God. Overcome fear with faith and trust. Sharpen your spiritual hearing by tuning more into the frequency of the spiritual realm, so you can discern God's voice from the noise of the world. Connect and build covenant relationships with like-minded Queens.

This is your Crowning Oil Unlock. Not everyone will understand it. But you'll never forget it. From this moment forward, you are not just called — you are crowned.

Closing Declaration – Sealed with Oil

As you rise from this sacred anointing encounter, may you never again question the value of your crushing or the richness of your royal identity. For out of it flowed the very oil that now crowns you for purpose. You are no longer the same. You are anointed, appointed, and aligned. The fresh oil that has been unlocked is not just for you, it's for the Kingdom, and for the lives you are called to impact, and for legacy.

Go forth with a renewed mind, a saturated heart, and the assurance that the God who anointed you in the secret place is now positioning you in divine spaces. You've been marked. You've been mantled. And this is just the beginning.

Let the oil speak. Sit with this reflection prayer. Say it aloud slowly.
Let it wash over you, not just as a promise, but as a present-tense reality.
This is not a future anointing. This is your right Now Oil.

Reflection Prayer: The Oil Is Here

Father, I receive the oil.
Not just a drop, but the overflow.
Not for display, but for divine deployment.

Let every place in me that has felt forgotten now feel fragrant with Your remembrance.

Let every dry place be saturated.

Let every weary "yes" be refreshed.

Let every past pain be met with present purpose.

I surrender to the sacred process.

I no longer strive — I soak.

I no longer chase — I choose to be chosen.

Let Your oil unveil the Queen in me.

Let my identity in you be sealed.

Let this anointing speak when I don't have the words.

Let it shine when I feel hidden.

Let it be strong even when I feel weak.

I am *crowned* in Your presence.

I am sealed by Your oil.

And I rise — not for applause, but for assignment.

In Jesus' name,
Amen.

Meditation Scriptures

Jeremiah 33:3

Psalm 5:3

1Thessalonians 5:17

2 Corinthians 5:17

NOTE PAGE
Crowning Insights and Revelations

CHAPTER 3

Crowning Oil for a Resilient Queen

"For if you remain silent at this time, liberation and rescue will arise for the Jews from another place, and you and your father's house will perish [since you did not help when you had the chance]. And who knows whether you have attained royalty for such a time as this [and for this very purpose]. "   -Esther 4:14

Royal Identity: The Raising of a Queen

God raises leaders, especially Queens, during times of crisis for every generation. These are women who recognize that the power to shift the trajectory of their lives, families, and communities does not rest in their position. Title or income level, but in their posture of surrender and submission to God and alignment with His Word and will.

God will take the initiative to execute His divine plan by searching for those who are willing to seek him, bear the cost, take the risk of carrying His vision, and sacrifice to fulfill His divine purpose. He is a great rewarder of those who diligently seek Him. (Hebrews 11:6)

The Esther Anointing

Consider Esther, an orphan, an ordinary girl, who was raised with a strong sense of identity, integrity, and grace. She was mentored by Mordecai, who instilled in her the wisdom, courage, and compassion that would later define her as a Queen. Esther's beauty radiated from within, and her humility, respectfulness, and accountability set her apart. Her authentic character, combined with her keen sense of timing, courage, and boldness, propelled her from the ordinary to the extraordinary.

Once upon a time, the King of Persia issued a royal decree, summoning the most beautiful virgins in the land to the palace so he could find a new Queen.

"Let us search the empire to find beautiful young virgins for the king... the young woman who most pleases the King will be made Queen." (Esther 2:2-4)

Esther was taken to the Palace and immediately obtained favor with the Supervisor over the Women's House. She was granted extra luxurious beauty preparations beyond her allowance. Top-level maidservants from the King's Palace were assigned to her, and she was moved to the best place in the house for women.

Her preparation process lasted twelve months, with six months of the oil of myrrh for purification, and another six months with oils, creams, and perfumes for beautification. She was prepared not just in appearance, but in spirit and identity. The oil of myrrh symbolized more than fragrance—it represented the purification of her heart and the spiritual preparation for her destiny.

When the appointed time arrived, Esther followed the advice of the Supervisor and approached the King with grace and confidence. At first sight, the King's heart was captivated, and he crowned her Queen that very night.

"The King loved Esther more than all the other women, and she obtained grace and favor in his sight more than all the virgins; so he set the royal crown upon her head and made her Queen." (Esther 2:17)

Esther had not yet revealed her true ethnicity or identity, or her family ties to Mordecai, as he had instructed her. When Mordecai uncovered a plot to wipe out the Jewish people, he turned to Queen Esther. Despite her initial hesitation, knowing that approaching the King without being summoned could result in death, Esther rose to the occasion with unwavering courage. She declared a sacred 3-day fast and prepared herself spiritually before boldly stepping into the King's chamber to expose the enemy's plan. (Esther 4:16)

Esther's surrender and obedience touched Heaven and shifted the destiny of her people. Her willingness to sacrifice comfort and security positioned her as a vessel of divine deliverance. Esther's story teaches us that favor follows obedience.

Your Sacred Season of Crowning

As you prepare to enter your sacred secret place with God, create a quiet, sweet spot dedicated to the presence and peace of God. Gather your oil, journal, and bible. Prepare to spend time in His presence and commune with the Holy Spirit. Be prepared to confront the enemy's opposition plans in prayer and take authority over the moment and your destiny.

This experience is intended to transform your heart, mind, and soul. It will help to prepare you to walk in clarity, confidence, and spiritual authority as a Queen.

The anointing will purify, heal, and empower you to step fully into your Kingdom identity as a resilient Queen. You are not just stepping into a role or clique, but you are stepping into dominion, power, and divine purpose.

Embrace Your Identity as a Queen

God is calling you to develop the same identity traits that defined Esther:

- A strong and elevated sense of royal identity in spite of humble beginnings.
- Integrity and authenticity
- Obedience and accountability
- Resilience, courage, and confidence
- Wisdom and servant leadership,
- Willingness to be mentored and to mentor others.

It will feel challenging at times. You may feel pressed and stretched, but that is part of the transformation process. Just as a diamond is formed under pressure, and just as oil is extracted through crushing, your trials are refining you for your mantle of royalty, authority, and service.

"We are hard pressed on every side, but not crushed; perplexed, but not in despair." (2 Corinthians 4:8)

You are being crowned for glory and anointed for divine impact. Every Queen must rule, reign, and thrive with persistent faith and resilience. Cultivate flexibility, adaptability, and perseverance. A Queen does not just survive adversity, she masters it.

Sweet Surrender and Alignment: Entering Your Divine Rest

Recognition, acknowledgment, forgiveness, surrender, and alignment are the starting points of all transformation experiences.

Enter into a place of sweet surrender, rest, and agreement with God. This is an opportunity to grow, change, and transform. Be willing to do the resilient inner work of identity, personal and leader development, healing, purification, cultivation for revelation, elevation, and manifestation. Uncover and release your voice, talents, gifts, God-given abilities, and allow the queen inside of you to show up.

As you do so, the Holy Spirit will reveal purpose, secrets, and strategies as you lean into his small still voice, nudges, dreams, and visions. (Proverbs 3:5-6 AMP)

This intimate, faith-driven, trustworthy anointing process prepares your heart and mind to enter into the divine rest of your soul, emotions, and spirit. In doing so, you become clearer, more concise, consistent, confident, and peaceful in your daily life.

Surrender starts with clarity: know your WHY and take the time to soak in this transformational anointing process. Give yourself the gift of sitting quietly, taking off the mask, resting, and simply BEING.

- Spend time on what really matters to you.
- Think about what you are thinking about.
- Separate from myths, misconceptions, and misalignments.
- Indulge in quietness, deep breathing, relaxation, and self-care and self-love, which are essential.
- Take a self-love journey on a healing path of discovery, deliverance, wholeness, and wellness.
- Rest is necessary. (Psalm 45:10)

Seven Types of Rest by Dr. Saundra Dalton Smith:

1. Physical Rest.
2. Mental Rest.
3. Sensory Rest.
4. Creative Rest.
5. Emotional Rest.
6. Social Rest.
7. Spiritual Rest.

See yourself the way He has always seen you. *"Alignment is a present state of being based on a past understanding and the future promise of who you will be."* Dr. Darnyelle Jervey Harmon

Transformation: The Purification Process

I invite you to enter into an anointed journey of surrender with God, releasing the cares of the world, letting go of what no longer serves you: anxieties, doubts, rejection, insecurities, and fears. This sacred journey calls you into a secret place of trust, release, divine rest, purification, l. wisdom, healing, and divine transformation. (Psalm 139:1-4)

Surrendering involves acknowledging, accepting, and appreciating God's authority in your life. As a loving Father, He sees and knows your heart, intentions, and He desires the best for you. This purification process allows God to search and cleanse your heart, remove the old, and renew you. It is a sacred exchange, releasing the past to receive His love, healing, validation, and the new thing. (Psalm 139:23-24)

Surrender calls for rest in his pure love, alignment, obedience, and action. Obedience requires faith and trust in Him. Seek Him for clarity and cultivate a personal, intimate relationship with Him.

In this sacred time, remove distractions, pray, visualize, journal, and meditate on His Word. The scriptures are alive and carry His breath and power. As you meditate on them, they will draw you closer to God and deepen your awareness of His presence. (Psalm 12:6)

God is about relationships, redemption, freedom, abundance, and destiny. His motives toward you are pure and intentional. This individualized purification process is about rediscovering your authentic self, loving yourself from the inside out, and loving God.

The Oil as a Purifier and Healer

The fresh oil of the Holy Spirit is a supernatural detoxifier, purifier, and healer. It cleanses and detoxifies impurities and removes the residue of brokenness, rejection, and contamination from past wounds and spiritual attacks. It will heal the root causes of identity issues and restore your sense of worthiness and wholeness.

The purification process can be both tangible and intangible—felt emotionally, spiritually, and physically. When you open your heart to the Holy Spirit's work, this process becomes revelatory and transformational. The anointing oil is symbolic of divine empowerment and preparation.

When her appointed time arrived, Esther found favor with everyone she encountered. Even the King was captivated by her at first sight. Defying custom, he did not send her back but instead crowned her as Queen. *(Esther 2:15-18)*

The Power of the Anointing

I have personally experienced God's healing and miracles. I have prayed, laid hands on others to impart the anointing of God, and witnessed the miraculous power of God. It is the wind of the Holy Spirit that carries us on eagles' wings into places of healing, deliverance, restoration, recovery, favor, promise, and destiny.

When you surrender, clarity will flow more consistently, and that clarity will empower you to operate with confidence and authority. Have faith that your Creator will do exceedingly and abundantly above all that you can think or ask. Trust that your steps are being divinely ordered. (Isaiah 40:31)

This anointing process is your preparation for greater. As you align with God's will and surrender to His refining, you will be crowned with resilience, authority. Rely on His strength, wisdom, and love. The oil upon your life signifies that God's grace and power flow and crown you with vision, strength, and favor. (Psalm 24:5)

My Personal Story: The Crushing that Produced the Oil

Diamonds are formed under immense pressure and heat during a crystallization process deep within the Earth's mantle. The intense heat and pressure cause carbon atoms to bond together in a specific crystalline structure, forming diamonds. Similarly, olives are crushed, pressed, and refined through a purification process to remove impurities, producing the precious and fragrant oil used for multiple purposes.

Both processes are intense, yet they produce something rare and valuable. Beauty is birthed through the crushing.

I know firsthand the crushing experience that produces oil for transformation. Over three decades ago, I suffered a life-altering moment when a hit-and-run accident left me critically injured and paralyzed. After enduring multiple surgeries, a year of intensive hospitalization in full-body mechanical traction, and months in a full-body cast, the doctors told my mother I would never walk again.

But through my mother's prayers and intercession, my unyielding faith, and a supernatural resilience, I not only regained my mobility two years later. Today, I can run, dance, and inspire others to overcome their own challenges.

During that pivotal season, my mother visited me every day after work. She prayed over me each night, anointed me with oil, and lovingly massaged my feet while singing hymns and reading scriptures to soothe my soul. Her sacrificial love, patience, and unwavering guidance infused me with comfort, encouragement, and the strength to endure.

This miraculous period became the defining moment when I surrendered my concerns, anxieties, and fears to God. It was in that surrender that I experienced a supernatural divine exchange; my pain for His peace, my fear for His faithfulness. Little did I know that this intense healing process was preparing and positioning me to receive the anointing oil of the Holy Spirit for a greater and more personal relationship with God.

My recovery and healing journey in the natural realm was long, intense, and painful. But now I see that my purpose, calling, and spiritual destiny were being forged in the spiritual realm at the same time. God was taking me from ashes to beauty. I look back with tears in my eyes and a heart full of gratitude, knowing now that the sovereign hand of God was upon my life.

I survived the crushing of the enemy of my soul. But I didn't just survive; I emerged out of the ashes carrying the fragrance and beauty of His presence. Hope and resilience became my superpower and an integral part of my prophetic mantle. But the anointing oil became my spiritual weapon, empowering me to know who I am. A woman of his divine grace equipped to love, build, create, train, transform, and reign with divine beauty and authority. The crushing produced my royal crown of resilience and positioned me to walk confidently in my prophetic assignment.

Tapping into the Anointing of the Holy Spirit and Divine Empowerment

"As for you, you have an anointing from the Holy One, and all of you know the truth." (1 John 2:20 AMP)

You Have Been Anointed to Reign

You have an anointing from the Holy One, and this oil carries the weight of Heaven's authority for generations to come. The Holy Spirit is not just a Gift, but you have been hand-selected to carry His oil, walk in divine empowerment, and reign with authority. You are not ordinary. You have been consecrated and set apart to reflect God's glory and operate in His power. This

Living in the Anointing

Do the internal work so that you are free, clear, and ready to dive deeper into revelation and empowerment. Be open and honest with yourself and surrender on purpose. Be willing to be vulnerable and share your concerns and desires with Him. (Psalm 139:23)

Make room in your heart and create a sacred space in your home to meet with Him for daily sweet communion. Keep your communication channels with God open; be intentional about listening for the "still small voice" of the Holy Spirit.

"Now if you will obey Me fully and keep My covenant, then out of all nations you will be My treasured possession." (Exodus 19:5)

Walk in Authority and Boldness

Obedience to His prompting takes faith. Respond wholeheartedly to every internal prompting and insight. The more you respond, the more He will reveal.

This oil is a divine weapon, a sacred crown, and a mantle of power. You have been called to reign, to walk in strength, and to manifest the Kingdom of God in the earth realm.

As Psalm 23:5 reminds us, "You anoint my head with oil," signifying that every opportunity, experience, and revelation in this sacred time is done at God's request. Yielding and surrendering to the Holy Spirit will position you to receive the resilient power of the anointing.

Queen, you have endured much not as a punishment, but as preparation. Every fiery trial was a prophetic classroom, and you passed each test with grace and victory. You are not the same woman who walked through the valley. You are stronger, wiser, and anointed.

Resilience is the crown you didn't know you were wearing while you were still hurting and bleeding. A resilient queen is not crowned by ease, she is crowned through endurance, obedience, and surrender to His will through the fire. Her oil doesn't just flow; it overflows because she allowed God to press, purify, and pour. The oil she carries is not cheap. It cost her everything that was not aligned with her purpose and destiny.

Every sleepless night, betrayal, loss, and delay were shaping a prayer warrior and a leading Queen. You weren't just surviving; you were *being crowned in the fire*. God is not only healing you, but He's also revealing you.

Your resilience has elevated you. Not only to reign, but to pour into others, into nations, and into legacy.

Your resilience is royal and Heaven approves of it. It is deeply spiritual. This chapter may close, but your resilience continues to speak. Let it speak in your posture, in your prayers, and your purpose. You are *crowned in resilience*, and your oil is not just for you. It's for the world you are called to impact.

Royal Reflection Questions:

1. What do you need to do to gain a more regal version of the royal you?

2. What foresight do you have for the future, and how can you position yourself for your desired outcomes?

3. What choices will you make to remove limiting mindsets and align with your true identity?

4. How do your relationships and community support or hinder your progress toward wearing your crown as a Kingdom Queen?

5. In what ways is your current identity impacting your journey toward your royal destiny? What sacrifices are you willing to make to step fully into your calling?

Activations/Action Steps

Everything that you need to grow in your Queendom is inside of you. As you flourish forward, I invite you to create your own Royal Crowning Consecration Plan.

1. As the original designer of your Queen's Court, what elements and supplies would you need to gather, organize, dedicate, and set up your sacred spiritual space for your consecration and transformation experience?

2. Napoleon Hill stated, "Change your mental attitude and the world around you will change accordingly." Imagine that you are designing a renewed, resilient state of mind through the power of the Word of God, self-care, and self-love. What would you do more of? What would you ask for more of during your time of prayer?

3. What is the one primary thing that you will need to do to come in greater alignment with the Word of God and the will of God for your life? What is the one thing that you can release to live a more yielded life?

4. What would it look like for you to incorporate surrender and alignment as a growth strategy for your personal development, business or marketplace ministry?

5. Simon T. Bailey stated, "Wisdom is knowing what to do while resilience is actually doing it." Resilience is sustained positive growth while adapting to disruptions. Keep in mind that resilience is a spiritual weapon. What does *resilience re-imagined* look like for you as you emerge as the Crowned Queen?

6. What might you gain if you focused on surrendering consistently in every area of your life?

7. Purchase your special Anointing Oil today.

Meditation Scripture

Luke 12:35 (NASB1995)
"Be dressed in readiness, and keep your lamps lit.

NOTE PAGE
Crowning Insights and Revelations

Bonus Gift
Who Is the Holy Spirit?

Having a relationship with the Holy Spirit is very personal, profound, and full of life-sustaining moments of encouragement and hope-filled promises. He promises you that He will never leave you or forsake you. The Holy Spirit longs to dwell within you. I encourage you to invite Him into every area of your life. You'll see a difference.

Open your heart to Him and receive all the benefits:

☐ His comfort.

☐ His truth.

☐ His grace.

☐ His leading.

☐ His guidance.

☐ His wisdom.

☐ His revelation and much more.

The Holy Spirit is faithful and gracious. Developing a relationship with Him is vital as you pursue, discover, and fulfill God's will for your life.

Who Is the Holy Spirit?

The Holy Spirit is the Spirit of Truth. He is the third person of the Holy Trinity (the Godhead). He is coequal with the Father and Son (Acts 5:3-4). He is the co-creator of the Universe. He is a gift from God sent to dwell with you and within you. He is the spirit of the living God, and He serves as:

☐ Your Comforter – He soothes your soul and brings peace in moments of uncertainty.

☐ Your Helper – He strengthens you when you feel weak and empowers you when you feel incapable.

☐ Your Guide/Teacher – He directs your steps and leads you into all truth.

☐ Your Advocate/Intercessor – He intercedes on your behalf before the throne of God.

He is like unto a harmless dove that descends from Heaven upon you as a visible demonstration of God's affirmation. He is the revealer of truth and our standby. (John 14-16 AMP)

Additional scripture references:

- ✓ **Luke 11:13**
- ✓ **Luke 4:1**
- ✓ **John 14:16-18**
- ✓ **John14:26**
- ✓ **Mark 1:10**
- ✓ **Luke 3:22**
- ✓ **John 1:32**
- ✓ **Mark 1:10**

He is omnipresent (Psalm 139: 7-10).

He is omniscient (I Corinthians 2:9-11).

He is omnipotent (Luke 1:35).

He empowers you, transforms you, and anoints you for your calling, purpose, assignment, and ministry. The oil of the Holy Spirit is symbolic of the "anointing oil." In the Old Testament, oil was representative of the Holy Spirit. The scriptures state that you shall anoint yourself with the anointing oil.

- ✓ **Exodus 29:7**
- ✓ **Exodus 40:9**
- ✓ **Exodus 30:22**

"Then you shall take the anointing oil and pour it on his head and anoint him."

(Exodus 29:7)

"You shall anoint Aaron and his sons, and consecrate them, that they may minister to Me as priests." (Exodus 30:30)

How Do You Receive the Holy Spirit?

By simply asking the Father for the infilling of the Holy Spirit. Ask boldly for the anointing of God. The Holy Spirit is the anointing. He is not hard to reach. He is already waiting for you to invite Him in.

Rise above the natural realm, above your emotions, thoughts, the noise, the desires of your flesh and will. Engage with the Father in the spirit realm. God is a spirit, and you must get in the spirit to find Him. (John 4:24)

The anointing oil is sacred and holy and the outpouring of it is to set you apart for divine purpose. When you receive the Holy Spirit, you are being set apart for God's work, positioned to carry His authority and reflect His glory.

Still Your Soul and Listen for the Voice of the Holy Spirit.

The more you acknowledge Him, the more you will begin to feel His influence. He is the source of your power. Invite Him into the details of your day. Acknowledge His presence at the start of each day and surrender your plans daily to Him.

He knows the desires of your heart, even the ones you haven't spoken aloud. Trust Him to lead you. Even when you can't see the way forward, He is already preparing the path.

"The Spirit of truth… will guide you into all truth." (John 16:13)

Approach Him with reverence and honor, for He is God. Quiet your heart and still your soul so you can hear when He speaks. He speaks through faint impressions, dreams, visions, circumstances, nature, other people, and through the Scriptures.

Often, He speaks in a small, still voice. He likes to court and woo you into His presence. He likes to engage your heart in conversation and worship.

Still your soul and listen for the voice of the Holy Spirit that will speak life-changing truth and give practical guidance day by day. He is trustworthy and faithful, so ask boldly and expect to hear from Him. No doubt, no hesitation. He will speak when the time is right.

- ✓ **John 15:26**
- ✓ **John 16:13-15**

- ✓ **Acts 22:4**

- ✓ **Acts 8:29**
- ✓ **Acts 10:19**
- ✓ **Acts 11:12**
- ✓ **Acts 13:2**
- ✓ **Acts 16:6-7**
- ✓ **I Timothy 4:1**
- ✓ **Hebrews 3:7**
- ✓ **Rev 2:7**

Be faithful and consistent in your ongoing dialogue and communion with the Holy Spirit. He is always present and a constant companion. Make it your desire to live in partnership with Him.

- o Speak to Him.
- o Listen to Him.
- o Obey Him.

Make Him a central and essential part of your life so you can experience the fullness of His guidance and power. Come before Him with humility, recognizing the weight of His presence. He is your strength in weakness, and your light in darkness. Be in tune with Him. Learn to recognize His still, small voice and wait patiently. His timing is perfect. Waiting allows you to receive wisdom in alignment with His will as you wear your Queen's Crown.

PART TWO

EMBRACING THE ANOINTING -

From Preparation to Purpose

"But you have been anointed by the Holy One, and you all have knowledge."

-1 John 2:20

CHAPTER 4

Crowning Oil for Financial Authority

"Cast your bread upon the waters, for you will find it after many days. Give a portion to seven, or even to eight, for you know not what disaster may come upon the land. If the clouds are full of water, they pour rain on the earth; and if a tree falls to the south or to the north, in the place where it falls, there it will lie. He who observes the wind will not sow, and he who regards the clouds will not reap. As you do not know the path of the wind, or how the body is formed in a mother's womb, so you cannot understand the work of God, the Maker of all things."   -Ecclesiastes 11:1-6 (AMP)

This chapter goes beyond the basic concepts of money. It is more about *financial mantles*, *multiplication*, and *mastery* of Kingdom finances, including giving, investing, spending, and stewarding.

2 Corinthians 9:8

"And God is able to make all grace abound toward you, that you, always having all sufficiency in all things, may have an abundance for every good work."

God is the ultimate giver. He has given us everything that we really need, on purpose, even His only Son, Jesus. His sacrificial giving helps you to understand the power of giving on purpose.

The scriptures declare, *"The earth is the Lord's, and everything in it—the world and all who live in it."* (Psalm 24:1) Everything belongs to God, yet He has granted mankind access to His divine treasures through faith, favor, and grace.

To secure your mantle of financial authority and dwell in your wealthy place, you first want to reassess and shift, if necessary, your money blueprint and mindset, develop a long-term financial plan, and cultivate a wealth consciousness. The mind is an extremely powerful tool for wealth-building and financial authority. A clear and sound mind, a healthy moncy blueprint, abundant intentions, generous attitudes, good stewardship, and financial authority to command the marketplace are necessary to manage the rich treasures given to you. It all begins in the depths of your mind. You may need to pray and ask God if there is a need for a spiritual money mindset transformation. Preparation will always come before elevation. Seek to understand how you feel about money. What are you saying about money? Do you have a giver's heart? Can you freely receive? As your mindset changes, and you trust and obey God, when it comes to giving, investing, and spending, your soul will prosper.

"I will give you the treasures of darkness and hidden riches in secret places, that you may know that I, the Lord, who call you by your name, am the God of Israel." (Isaiah 45:3)

Money is not just currency used to create an exchange; it is an instrument, a tool constantly in motion seeking purpose and destination. Without a vision, money and wealth, lack direction, and it has nowhere to land. It must be guided with purpose, positioned for impact, and stewarded wisely for financial legacies.

Consciousness of any type is defined as "the state of being awake and aware of one's surroundings." Wealth consciousness is a state of mind where you feel abundant, regardless of your current financial status. Expand your awareness of the wealth that exists within every part of your being. Be economically woke and aware of where money resides, how to acquire it, how to grow it, how to protect it, and how to transfer it to the next generation.

Financial vision, strategic goals, good stewardship, financial leverage, collaborations, and nurtured relationships are non-negotiables of a wealth-building plan. Good management and true authority require intentionality, responsibility, systems, and capital. As the scripture reminds us: *"To whom much is given, much is required."* (Luke 12:48)

Your willingness to exercise faith, invest, persevere, build, establish, create, leverage, engage, and instruct is the core foundation of your royal court. As I pointed out in *The 10 Commandments of the Wealth Transfer*, wealth and money must have purpose and direction—they require a plan and strategy to multiply and flow effectively in your life.

God has already endowed you with the power to create wealth (Deuteronomy 8:18), not just for yourself, but to transform your family, build generational blessings and wealth, and expand the Kingdom of God.

Divine wealth is wisdom! A conscious and creative perspective backed by faith, purpose-driven actions, million-dollar habits, and unshakable persistence to see visions to fruition. Wealth is multi-dimensional, and it is more than money; it is a creative force, a choice, a commitment to divine excellence and financial authority on purpose.

Financial authority is the bold refusal to be intimidated by lack, poverty, injustice, and systematic inequities. It is the relentless pursuit of wisdom and knowledge, clear strategies, alignment, stability, and prosperity— manifesting in health, healing, abundance, wealth, and wholeness in mind, body, soul, and spirit. Establish sacred core values, a plan for economic preparation or recovery, financial freedom, and wealth creation. Be a giver, sow financial seeds, and be of service to others.

Ownership, financial independence, and wealth equal freedom.

It is a choice to surrender your life to a higher commitment and a greater goal to serve. Being true to who you were created to be and self-sustaining will require a shift in your subconscious money beliefs and a re-positioning of your blueprint, re-establishing cultural norms and family values. You must refuse to be held back by lack, low income, or racial injustice. This will take faith, alignment, courage, and support. Moving forward with truth, a vision for your financial legacy, tireless passion, a financial plan, self-determination, and energy to create both intangible and tangible assets.

Are You Ready for the Wealth Transfer?

The $68 Trillion Wealth Transfer: A Generational Window of Opportunity...

"No one can prosper when they expect to remain poor."
Maggie Lena Walker

According to multiple reports, including a notable analysis featured in Forbes, the impending wealth transfer is estimated to reach **$68 trillion by 2030**. This unprecedented shift, driven by intergenerational change, is not merely a financial historical event; it's a divine opportunity for Kingdom Queens to step into a legacy of authority, abundance, influence, and prosperity. As you prepare to wield financial authority, remember that the abundance God promises is both tangible and intangible.

"But you shall remember the Lord your God, for it is He who gives you power to get wealth..."
(Deuteronomy 8:18)

To reign in the area of financial authority, you must be delivered from the spirit of *fear, scarcity,* and *the love of money.* True financial authority is not about counting numbers or how much you have; it's about how much authority and dominion you walk in over beliefs, mindsets, systems, and spiritual forces that try to limit you or take you out.

Practical Financial Keys to Financial Planning, Building and Stewarding Generational Wealth

- **Will and Trust – estate planning and legacy blueprint -**

  A Queen who reigns with wisdom must prepare for life beyond the throne with estate planning and tax planning. This requires you to secure your legacy. A properly executed Will and Trust ensures that your assets and brilliance, including real estate, 401(k), intellectual property, business interests, non-profits, investments, pension, insurance, trademarks, registrations, and certifications, are protected and passed on with intention and not confusion. It's not just about assets; it's about legacy. *Make power moves and secure an estate plan with your attorney that will ensure the seamless transfer of assets.*

  The Will is a declaration of your desires after

death. The Trust agreement is a blueprint for distribution and protection. In addition, I suggest that you have a Healthcare Directive and Durable Power of Attorney created. These are tools that support your wishes and position your lineage for peace, clarity, and dominion.

"A good man leaves an inheritance to his children's children..." — Proverbs 13:22

Reflection Prompt: Will and Trust

What values, wisdom, or spiritual truths do I want to preserve and pass on to my children's children? Am I being intentional about putting my affairs in order for the next generation, or avoiding difficult conversations about legacy planning? Who will control my estate?

- **Creditworthiness – the testimony of trust**
  Credit is not just about scores—it's about credibility. Your ability to be trusted with small doors often determines the size of the next one God opens. Cultivating strong credit isn't just financial—it's spiritual. It reflects how you

manage what has been placed in your hands. Build wisely. Protect fiercely. Steward consistently. Your creditworthiness is a financial testimony of your integrity, discipline, and preparedness to scale.

Reflection Prompt: Creditworthiness

What does my current financial behavior reveal about my ability to be trusted with more?

Where can I become more diligent, disciplined, or responsible to elevate my financial credibility and prepare for divine doors?

- **Life Assurance – provision beyond presence**
  While the world sees life *insurance* as a financial backup plan, we understand it as a strategic assurance of protection for your legacy. Life assurance is love in action—an invisible seed that blooms for your family in your absence. It is a prophetic gesture of stewardship and foresight. It says: "Even in my departure, I still provide."

Queens plan ahead, not out of fear, but from a place of wisdom, protection, and honor.

Reflection Prompt: Life Assurance

If I transitioned tomorrow, what would my financial footprint say about the love and preparation I've left behind?

Have I ensured that those I love are protected, covered, and provided for, even in my absence?

- **Infrastructure and Systems – sustaining the flow**

  Every royal palace requires structure and support. You cannot pour new wealth into old wineskins. If you desire an overflow, you must prepare the vessel. This includes long-term financial planning, solid financial systems, digital tools, operational processes and procedures, support, and trusted advisors to support the flow and multiplication of your resources. Systems sustain what the oil starts. Without infrastructure and systems, visions leak and limit your capacity to grow and scale. Learn to document to duplicate, which will help position you to prosper. The future requires not just faith, but framework and pillars.

Reflection Prompt: Infrastructure & Systems

What structures or systems do I need to create, improve, or delegate in order to better sustain the wealth and wisdom God has entrusted to me?

Are there gaps, inefficiencies, or missed opportunities in how I manage my resources, time, or team?

Building sustainable wealth is a multi-generational journey.

"Wealth is a team sport, and most of your teammates are not yet alive." *Dr. Boyce Watkins*

Foundational Truths and Disciplines of Financial Authority

Your relationship with wealth and money is a direct reflection of your faith, understanding, structures, discipline, and the intentions of your heart. Financial authority is not just about accumulation, but about alignment with divine principles, wise stewardship, and intentional action.

There are principles, spiritual laws, financial concepts, and systems that govern the manifestation of financial prosperity, wealth transfer, and kingdom resources. When you align with these principles, you activate supernatural access to abundance, opening heavenly portals that pour out divine increase.

Below are key foundational truths and disciplines to support your Kingdom financial authority:

1. Purpose-driven Faith: passionate belief and focus

To walk in financial independence and authority, you must first walk in unwavering belief, faith, and focus. Your purpose and passion fuel expansion and growth. When you align your finances with God's purpose, steward your resources with integrity, and create with an abundance mindset, you become an agent of transformation, not only for your own life but for generations to come.

- **A faithful, prayerful, productive lifestyle** and **a financial plan** removes fear, eliminates the paralysis of failure, and sets you up for long-term success.
- A **disciplined mindset** and self-mastery allow you to sit still, hear the voice of God, and receive divine wisdom and direction.
- A **servant leader's heart** seeks to add truth, value, knowledge, and transformation in the lives of others.
- A **Kingdom-driven mindset** embraces abundance and legacy, refusing to be limited by external circumstances and failure to plan.

2. Wealth Begins in the Mind: the power of a renewed money mindset and rewired subconscious money beliefs

Wealth is first conceived in the mind before it manifests in the natural world. Transforming financial reality requires transforming thought life. Allow the Word of God, His principles, and spiritual laws to take root in your consciousness and subconscious mind.

- **Release Limiting Beliefs** – Overcome fear, anxiety, and unworthiness regarding wealth and money management.
- **Forgiveness as a Gateway** – Unforgiveness creates blockages; financial flow is connected to emotional healing and spiritual release.
- **Identity in Abundance** – You are a divine Kingdom Heir. You are worthy of abundance and prosperity. Abundance is not external, it is your birthright, woven into your Kingdom DNA.
- **Faith-Filled Financial Thinking** – Invest in you, your business, and your team. Your words and thoughts have power:
  - *"As a man thinketh in his heart, so is he."* (Proverbs 23:7)
  - *"You shall decree a thing, and it shall be established for you."* (Job 22:28)

3. Financial Stewardship & Accountability: the gateway to financial dominion and generational wealth

God has entrusted you with financial authority, but stewardship is required to sustain and multiply His resources. Financial authority and wealth are not measured in terms of possessions or money, but in values, mission, passion, relationships, service, solutions, and fulfillment.

- **Spiritual Law of Sowing and Reaping** – The principle of seedtime and harvest is a Kingdom mandate. (*Galatians 6:7*)
- **Financial Stewardship** – Honor God through wise management of your resources, sowing, and giving:
  - Save diligently and spend intentionally. (Proverbs 11:25)
  - Give generously: including tithes & offerings. (Luke 6:38)

What changes in your lifestyle or mindset are needed to fully embrace your financial reign and authority?

Personal Conviction and Spiritual Legacy

For eight years, I have poured oil upon countless others, serving, coaching, anointing, and crowning women in their divine royalty as graduates of my signature coaching program – "Game-Changer." Yet, in this sacred crowning year, the oil flowing from these pages is not just an overflow offering, but it is the costly result of my own crushing, refining, transforming, and ultimate next-dimension elevation.

Heaven crowned me in my most tender and vulnerable moments of tears, trauma, silent suffering, great needs, unseen battles, medical crises, and heart-wrenching sacrifices. The crucible of pain was not my breaking; it was my *Becoming*. Thank God, there is always a rainbow after the storm.

It forged an unshakable mantle of resilience and kingdom authority upon my life, positioning me to reign boldly as a transformational leader, spiritual strategist, and prophetic voice in the marketplace.

The oil of resilience and financial authority lies richly upon my life, granting grace and favor in my endeavors, enlargement of my brand, and expansion of my borders. You do not change out of your comfort zone. You change when you are uncomfortable and shift.

Now, this fresh Oil is yours to receive, not just as a blessing, but as a prophetic Charge. You are called to carry, release, and create with it. This is not just a moment; it is a divine mandate. The greatest wealth transfer in history is upon us, and you have been chosen to steward it. With God's authority resting upon you, you can command your wealth and live in your wealthy place. Step forward. Take your place.

Queen, you were never meant to chase wealth — you were chosen to *carry* it. The $68 trillion wealth transfer is not a myth or some market projection; it is a divine movement, and you are being summoned to steward a portion of it with intentionality, purpose, and power.

As you align your belief systems, renew your financial mindset, and embrace disciplined stewardship, you are unlocking more than provision — you are unlocking legacy. Your financial authority begins with personal conviction and culminates in spiritual inheritance. It's not just about what flows to you, but what flows *through* you to generations.

This is your coronation moment — to stand, not as a beggar hoping for a breakthrough, but as a builder of wealth streams, a Kingdom investor, and a Kingdom financier. You are *anointed* for this. You are *positioned* for this. You are *crowned* for this.

Now rise, prevail, create wealth, and build your legacy on purpose with authority.

Royal Reflections and Call to Action

Take a moment to reflect deeply on the following questions:

- **Leadership and Legacy Vision:** Be clear about your overall vision and financial goals. Put your future self first and create a life that you love and that serves others. *Think like a Queen and act like a CEO.* Develop an investment plan and make long-term investments. How does building generational wealth align with your divine identity as a Kingdom Queen? What intentional steps will you take to establish and pass on this legacy?

- **Personal Alignment:** What is your money story? In what areas of your financial life are you out of alignment? What adjustments can you make to become a better steward of the wealth and resources entrusted to you?

- **Healing & Release:** Develop a financial wellness plan. Are there any past mistakes or lessons that you feel are blocking your happiness or financial success? Do you find it difficult to forgive yourself? How might releasing these burdens free you to step fully into abundance?

- **Money Mental Shifts & Self-Mastery:** Is there a need for a money reset? What limiting beliefs, fears, or past money narratives do you need to release to walk fully in your financial authority? Are you able to generate multiple income streams from the things you own? Can you pass these things on to your children?

- **Spiritual Clarity:** Choose to be a Queen of your financial future. Do you find it hard to quiet your mind when you try to pray about your financial wellness? How can you create space for divine wisdom and clarity in your financial journey?

- **Positioning for Wealth:** Create multiple income streams. Are you properly positioned to receive, manage, and multiply wealth? Are you a generous giver? Do you tithe ten percent (10%) of your income to God? If not, what strategic moves must you make to step into divine alignment?

- **Action Steps:** Create a long-term financial plan with detailed strategies outlined in a financial roadmap, setting you up for sustainable growth and success. Money needs a legacy. What bold, intentional steps will you take this week to expand your financial authority, financial legacy, cultivate abundance, and move toward generational wealth?

Without a financial management system and team, you will find it challenging to reach your financial independence, authority, and the full potential of your throne and calling. Pray and command your resources daily because lack and poverty are a curse. Know your purpose, mission, and numbers. Pursue inner excellence, serve others, add great value; and money, wealth, and abundance will find you. Build a strong support system. Take the courage to do what it takes. Believe that you can make a difference.

Now is your time to rise and flourish. Release that which is no longer serving you and get in your sweet space to flow in this race. Thrive in the process of growth and change. The crowning oil for financial independence and authority has been poured. Walk in obedience, move with resilience, and embrace the wealth that is rightfully yours. Step into your financial authority with a heart ready to embrace the wealth that is your birthright. The crown is waiting, will you step into it? Remember, information without action is a waste of time.

Closing Prayer: A Crowned Steward's Prayer

Father, I thank You for trusting me with the gifts, resources, streams, opportunities, and plans. Today, I surrender my finances, my future, and my family legacy back into Your hands. I purpose in my heart to be a generous giver and tither. For you give seed (money) to the sower (giver).

Purify my heart and align my mind with inner excellence. Teach me to steward with wisdom, multiply with integrity, and build with divine strategy. Guide me and direct me as I develop a trustworthy money circle of professional providers and advisors.

Let the oil of financial planning and authority rest upon me, crowned not only with favor but with discipline, accountability, and clarity. I decree that I am a lender and not a borrower, a creator of wealth and not a carrier of lack. I break every adverse agreement and generational curse of lack, poverty, debt, and financial assault, and I step boldly into generational blessing and prophetic provision.

Anoint my decisions to invest wisely. Bless the work of my hands as I create multiple streams of income. Let every resource connected to my assignment be released, and financial opportunities be fulfilled.

I am aligned, anointed, and appointed to prosper for my future self, your glory, and generations to come.

In Jesus' name,
Amen.

Meditation Scripture

Dcutcronomy 28:12 (AMP)
"The Lord will open for you His good treasure house, the heavens, to give rain to your land in its season and to bless all the work of your hand; and you will lend to many nations, but you will not borrow."

NOTE PAGE

Crowning Insights and Revelations

CHAPTER 5

Crowning to Reign

"For if, because of one man's trespass, death reigned through that one, much more will those who receive abundance of grace and the free gift of righteousness reign in life through the One, Jesus Christ." —Romans 5:17

From Anointing to Reigning

Queen, you are the anointed gift, crowned in courage, forged in faith, and strengthened by the embodiment of inner excellence and resilience. Your transformation journey from surrendering to anointing to reigning is an ongoing, evolving, inner style and intimate growth process. The anointing of the Holy Spirit is the difference that makes the difference.

Once you are crowned with his rich anointing, you are seated and sealed in the Kingdom's identity, authority, and power. Every tear you have shed has been transformed into rare diamonds and a radiant testament to your legacy journey. You were not just born to survive; you were destined to reign and thrive.

You are positioned to govern and reign in your court with wisdom, clarity, and unshakable confidence. Stand in your divine authority. Refuse to tolerate dishonor and disrespect, never allow anyone to mishandle your crown.

Hold fast to the faith that carried you this far, and do not cast your crown away. When no one else believes, believe in yourself. Each day is a divine invitation to rise higher, embrace new opportunities, and expand your influence. Growth is not optional; it is the foundation of sustained success.

Wear your crown with love and dignity. Rule and reign with unwavering grace. Reach and fulfill your undeniable genius zone on your throne.

Walk like a legend. Speak life. Love with intention. Seek wisdom. Pursue divine connections, covenant relationships, and special opportunities. You were never meant to shrink, you were born to establish, to expand, and to build your prophetic legacy. You are never alone. The throne is yours, and wealth has been assigned to you on purpose.

Embracing Your Prophetic Legacy

Queen, the time has come for you to step fully into the destiny God has prepared for you. You are now carrying the crown of divine identity. The sacred anointing oil has been poured upon your life. You stand at the threshold of a New Beginning. A place where faith, focus, and divine positioning will lead you into a realm of influence, impact, and legacy.

Walk fully in your divine mandate and build a prophetic legacy that transcends generations. The oil that consecrated you is not just a symbolic blessing, it is an eternal impartation of spiritual covering, authority, power, and divine positioning. You are called to lead, influence, and transform, not just for yourself, but for those assigned to your prophetic mantle.

True reigning is not about a title, it is about transformation. It is about standing unapologetically in your anointing, refining your gifts, fortifying your relationships, and aligning your life with the Kingdom's purpose. This requires a commitment to authenticity, divine wisdom, sacred self-care and self-love, and covenant relationships that support your continued growth and elevation.

To sit in your royalty, authority, and to reign effectively, embrace our C.R.O.W.N. Mandate:

C.R.O.W.N. – The Five Pillars of Royal Purpose-Driven Leadership

- **C – Change:** Transformation is non-negotiable. As you shift and ascend, you must continually evolve, shedding and releasing old mindsets, fears, and limitations. True Queens embrace change as the birthing ground for elevation, leadership, and domination.

- **R – Resilience:** The crown is not for the faint of heart. Your strength is forged in the fire of trials and refined through perseverance, prayer, and fasting. Like Queen Esther, you are called for such a time as this—rise boldly in the renewal of your mind, heart, and spirit.

- **O – Oil:** Your anointing is your healing and divine distinction. The outpouring of oil upon your life is consecrated and costly. It will open you to divine favor and opportunities. It carries the fragrance of your crushing and the weight of your assignment. Allow yourself to be used by God. Walk in it with honor and learn to *receive* the blessings of the anointing.

- **W – Wisdom:** Queen Sheba is renowned for her wisdom and discernment. She pursued the King for wisdom and understanding. She left his presence a changed woman and left a legacy of influence and wealth. Seek divine wisdom daily, for it will establish your throne and safeguard your reign.

- **N – Now:** Your time is NOW. Stay focused. No more waiting. No more doubting or second-guessing. No more feelings of unworthiness. Step forward in bold obedience and focused leadership to create and build your prophetic legacy. Nurture the legacy you are called to build.

Walking in Your Royal Authority

Reigning is not solely about personal surrender and personal empowerment; it is also about education, excellence, and legacy. Just as Queen Esther was mentored by Mordecai and Queen Sheba was taught by King Solomon, you must surround yourself with wise counsel and mentorship.

Make it a priority to cultivate covenant relationships that fuel your purpose, receive the outpouring of Mentors, and pour into others with in. The anointing oil is not just a temporary act of adornment but an internal reminder that you are empowered to lead, influence and impact.

- **Authenticity:** Fully embrace the calling, unique gifts, purpose, and strengths that God has invested and entrusted to you. Exercise your gifts. Affirm your identity by immersing yourself in the Word of God, allowing it to renew and shift your perspective, sharpen your spiritual hearing, and refine your strategies. Speak your truth. Your authenticity is your crown—it sets you apart to shine as a genuine and compassionate source of light and love.

- **Sacred Self-Care & Self-Love:** A true regal Queen understands that her well-being is vital and non-negotiable. Prioritize daily spiritual, emotional, and physical nourishment so that you can reign from a place of overflow. Declare the promises of God over your life. Like Queen Esther, practice the art of self-care and replenish your spirit daily through prayer and meditation on the Word of God.

- **Building Relationships & Mentorship:** The greatest Queens do not reign alone, but they hold themselves accountable to their leaders. Invest in meaningful covenant connections and relationships, align with wisdom-filled mentors, and pour into the next generation of Kingdom Queens. Like the Queens in the Old Testament, take the time to sit at the feet of wise counsel.

Abundance is your birthright, and your throne is waiting. Embrace your inheritance so your unfolding generational blueprint is well established with wisdom and grace. The power of life and death is in your tongue. Boldly solidify your state of affairs, for you are **Crowned to Reign.**

"If we endure, we will also reign with Him."
-2 Timothy 2:12 (AMP)

Crowned to Reign:

A Redeeming Prophetic Declaration

and Affirmation of Power and

Purpose *(Inspired by Isaiah 61)*

I Am Crowned to be an Anointed Kingdom Queen

Anyone can become a queen because anyone can love and serve. But to be chosen, set apart, and anointed for such a time as this is a royal calling.

I am a Queen anointed to proclaim, create, build, heal, transform, establish, and expand the Kingdom. The oil upon my life is not by accident; it has been pressed, purified, and poured out through my journey of faith. Every tear, every trial, and every triumph have prepared me for my divine assignment.

The Holy Spirit's anointing upon my life empowers me to speak the "truth in love" and perform divine tasks beyond my capacity.

I walk in great faith, my trust unwavering, my purpose undeniable. My pain has been converted into purpose, my vulnerabilities into strength, and my authenticity into power. I am not bound by fear or past mistakes. I break barriers with boldness and humility, clothed in wisdom and led by the Spirit.

I am the embodiment of resilience and grace, walking in the fullness of my Kingdom identity. I move with precision, discernment, and divine alignment, ready to release the impact I was created to bring forth.

I Am Crowned to Reign with Authority

I am not just called and chosen, but I am commissioned to and reign and thrive. I step boldly into my divine authority, seated in power and dominion. The Kingdom of Heaven backs me, and I move with confidence, knowing that no weapon formed against me shall prosper.

I lead with courage without compromise, stand firm in my convictions, and speak life into every room I enter. I am divinely inspired, leveraging wisdom and strategy to build, bless, and break through. Generational wealth is assigned to my throne. I am a divine steward, multiplying and manifesting abundance for those who come after me.

I do not shrink; I do not second-guess. I rise unapologetically, and I embrace my position as a Kingdom Queen. My reign is righteous, my faith is unbreakable, my influence is undeniable, and my legacy is unstoppable.

I Am Crowned for His Glory

I am royalty. I am a master of my unique gifts. I am brilliance personified. My life is a reflection of God's glory, and my impact is an extension of His divine purpose. I walk with excellence, integrity, and unwavering faith, knowing that the crown I wear is a testament to His faithfulness.

I celebrate the greatness within me, honoring the gifts, talents, and wisdom He has placed in my hands. I embrace my uniqueness, my voice, and my story, using them as instruments of transformation and empowerment. My heart is full of His joy, grace, and peace. I shall proclaim the praises of the Lord.

I decree and declare that I will not just exist—I will thrive and live in an abundance of faith, relationships, resources, strategies, and favor. The windows, gates, and portals of heaven are open. I will not just build, I will establish. I will not just lead, I will leave a lasting legacy. My crown is secure, my purpose is clear, and my destiny is unstoppable.

I am crowned for glory, for the Lord shall be my everlasting light.

Royal Reflections and Call to Action: Step Boldly into Your Queendom

Queen, this is your moment, and your mourning has been turned into joy and your ashes into beauty. The oil has been poured, refreshing your soul, the crown has been placed, and the charge has been given. You are no longer waiting for permission—

You Are Commissioned to Reign!

Use your anointing, your story, and your voice to impact your family, community, and beyond. Your voice is a powerful tool to shift the atmosphere to bring about change.

Take time to reflect on these questions as you fully embrace your prophetic legacy:

- **Legacy Activation:** Why are you unique? What will be your legacy? What will be the evidence of your reign? What changes in your lifestyle or mindset are needed to fully embrace your reign?

How will your life, leadership, and influence shape the generations to come?

- **Divine Authority:** What will be your crowning moment? Are you fully walking in your power, or are you still shrinking in spaces where you were meant to shine? How will you exercise and maintain your spiritual authority?

- **Sacred Stewardship:** How are you managing your gifts, talents, and resources? What changes do you need to make to align your financial, spiritual, and emotional wealth with God's kingdom agenda?

- **Prophetic Boldness:** What is God calling you to build, release, or declare in this season? What do you desire to create in the next five years?

- **Commitment to the Call:** What bold step will you take today to fully embrace your identity as a Kingdom Queen? What daily practices will you implement to sustain your reign? How do you plan to guard your anointing and your crown against the corrosion and challenges of the world? Will you join our Movement?

When you guard your heart, take care of your temple, and nurture your spirit daily, you protect your anointing and set the stage for continual divine empowerment and blessings.

Your Time Is Now!

No more delays. No more doubts. No more waiting. You were created for such a time as this to build, to bless, and to break through. **Rise up and reign!**

You have been anointed to reign — not just to survive, but to *thrive in divine authority*. This is more than a chapter. It's a *clarion call*. A spiritual activation. A sacred shift from waiting for validation to walking in consecrated dominion.

No longer will you hide your brilliance, question your mantle, or shrink under the weight of your calling. You have been *called forth* as a royal daughter — clothed in strength, crowned in glory, and commissioned with prophetic fire.

Every lesson, every oil press, every healing moment has led to this divine intersection: *Reign boldly. Lead righteously. Build prophetically.* You are not just carrying legacy — you *are* the legacy.

Queen, the crown placed upon you is your divine authorization.

Now rise. Take your seat at the table prepared for you in the presence of your enemies, and reign like A Crowned Queen.

Personal Prophecy:
A Divine Release of the Queen's Crown

Dearest Queen:

Allow me to speak into your life…I announce, declare, decree, and prophesy that your days of resistance, opposition, and struggle are over. For strong and resilient winds of change, excellence and favor are blowing to uproot and up-level.

LIVE on purpose with inner strength and excellence, embrace your calling and new opportunities, and reign with undeniable wisdom and unshakeable power. You have been given permission and authority to shine in your brilliant zone. As you allow the world to see your excellence and elegance as a Kingdom Queen, you shall experience more grace, beauty, favor, wealth, wisdom, and the glory of God.

Set your intentions, for it's a New Day! You have entered a new season of momentum, transformation, and acceleration! God shall grant the desires of your heart. He shall amplify your vision and multiply your streams of income. The oil of the Holy Spirit shall never run dry, and in Him you shall be strong and sweet. Your crown of glory and joy shall shine brightly, your inner excellence illuminating every path you create and walk upon.

WEALTH COMES NOW. I decree great showers of blessings, protection, and ridiculous favor to be your double-portion. I declare that your Crown of Legacy shall be marked by deep authenticity, excellence, unwavering authority, and divine rewards.

QUEEN, rise brilliantly, dare to place your crown upon your head, believe in you, stand strong in your convictions, excellence and values, speak the truth courageously, and set others FREE ... for you shall Bloom and Prosper as a trailblazing pioneer with A Queen's CROWN.

I release it by faith in Jesus' name.

Complete the inner work and healing, go forth, Anointed One.

Amen.

Submitted by Dr. Lougenia J. Rucker
Divine Diamonds Ministries, Apostle
www.divinediamondsministries.ning.com

"Blessed be the LORD your God who delighted in you to set you on the throne..." (I Kings 10:9 AMP)

NOTE PAGE
Crowning Insights and Revelations

PART THREE
RISE & REIGN –
Royal Authority and Generational Legacy

Blessed [fortunate, prosperous, and favored by God] is the man who fears the Lord [with awe-inspired reverence and worships Him with obedience], Who delights greatly in His commandments. His descendants will be mighty 45don earth; The generation of the upright will be blessed. Wealth and riches are in his house, and his righteousness endures forever.

Psalm 112:1-3

CHAPTER 6

Crowning to Serve

"But whoever would be great among you must be your servant, and whoever would be first among you must be your slave."

-Matthew 20:26-27 (ESV)

As a Queen crowned with divine authority and grace, it's important to understand that your crown was never meant to be a symbol of privilege, but a mantle of *service*. The call to reign is intertwined with the call to serve, for true royalty reflects the heart and love of God, who came not to be served but to serve. Your crown is a sacred vessel to bless, build, and empower those you serve.

This chapter will guide you into a deeper understanding of how your authority and influence are meant to uplift and inspire others, minister to needs, and serve God's purpose on earth. Your crown equips you, not for self-exaltation, but for *servant leadership*, which is the highest form of authority in the Kingdom of God.

The beloved, Dr. Rev. Martin Luther King, Jr. endured beatings and hardships, turned a cheek to degradation, put up with indecency, tolerated inequities, and withstood oppression so that he may serve mankind. Dr. King literally changed the racial, economic, and political direction of our world.

The Heart of a Queen: Embracing Service

As a Queen of Faith, you are called to a powerful role of influence and impact. You are anointed to carry the burdens of others to the altar of God. You are appointed to bring about transformation through the power of the anointing of the Holy Spirit upon your life. Your services and products are designed to empower others. The anointing you carry is not just for your personal well-being but is also meant to be poured out to heal, restore, and inspire others. The anointing demonstrates strength, strategy, wisdom, grace, gratitude, respect, and kindness.

It searches for and seeks innovative ideas and insights that make this world better for the next generation. This is the heart of a true Queen, one who rises not just for personal gain, but to see others thrive and flourish as well.

Royalty Through Service

There is a chaotic and dark world crying for peace, stability, and enlightenment. There is a lost world crying out for something to connect to and to belong to. The world is waiting for your gifts, talents, God-given abilities, and your services. You get to make a choice. You get to decide to choose you. A person of deep values, a person of excellence, and a commitment to serve.

Commit yourself to do the right thing, at the right time, in the right way, and with the right people. Help to develop a culture that appreciates, generates, and retains wealth and prosperity. Service is about making a difference, making an impact, and influencing others in the next generation. In addition, add great value that enhances the well-being of others and an attitude of grace to your service, and you will embody royalty through service.

When you embrace your crown, accept the calling to serve as a marketplace leader, a mentor, and a businesswoman who is divinely placed in the lives of others for a reason and a season. The divine oil upon your head is not only for your own advancement but to equip you for service, whether it's in your home, your workplace, your business/ministry, your community, or beyond.

Service is the pathway through which your authority is validated. You lead not by command but by the strength of your actions and the grace with which you serve. Serving others reveals the true nature of the Kingdom of God, where greatness is not measured by power, but by surrender and humility.

The Power of Influence: Serving with Grace

Proverbs 4:9 (AMP)

"She will place on your head a garland of grace; She will present you with a crown of beauty and glory."

You are not called to serve not out of obligation but out of *divine grace,* which is God's undeserved favor. He adds honor, protection, provision, and love with His favor. As you serve, you grow in favor and grace, drawing others to the truth of God's Kingdom. Grace and favor will find you as you diligently seek good and find the opportunities to serve (Proverbs 11:27). Your crown is an invitation to extend His Kingdom into the earth by demonstrating the *power of influence and resilience.* The way you lead, the way you serve, and the way you interact with others will reflect the love and mercy of God.

A Resilient Queen will be blessed by God's favor and grow in grace, thrive, bear good fruit, and prosper in life. She will flourish and be fresh and rich in contentment. (Psalm 92:14)

This royal influence allows you to lead in kindness, serve in a way that shifts cultures, breaks barriers, provides solutions, and opens doors for others. Your influence will reach far beyond your immediate circles, touching hearts, minds, and lives, and paving the way for God's purpose to unfold through you.

The Divine Responsibility of Service

To wear a Queen's crown is an honor and divine responsibility. Take one step at a time to walk in ministry to serve others with wisdom, compassion, and understanding as you walk in your royal authority. You will be graced and empowered to recover every ounce of hope that may have leaked out because of past issues or challenges.

The more you serve with humility, the more you will witness God's favor upon your life. The scripture says, he gives grace to the humble. (Proverbs 3:34)

Your influence is a gift from God, one that you must steward well. Service is not about what you can gain, but about what you can give. You were crowned and empowered for such a time as this.

Embracing Your Role as a Servant Leader

The greatest leaders are those who serve selflessly, who lead with grace, compassion, and understanding. This is the type of leadership that attracts the favor of God.

To serve with grace, embrace the following principles:

1. **Humility:** A servant leader doesn't elevate herself above others but leads by example. True Queens know that they are first called to serve, not to be served. Humility always comes before honor and rewards. (Proverbs 18:12)

2. **Empathy:** A servant leader understands the needs of others and meets them with a heart of compassion and action. Ephesians 5:2 (AMP) " ...and walk *continually* in love [that is, value one another—practice empathy and compassion, unselfishly seeking the best for others], just as Christ also loved you and gave Himself up for us, an offering and sacrifice to God [slain for you, so that it became] a sweet fragrance. "

3. **Empowerment:** True service isn't about doing everything for others, but equipping them to rise, to become empowered, and to walk in their own calling. Luke 21:19 (AMP) "By your [patient] endurance [empowered by the Holy Spirit] you will gain your souls.

4. **Sacrifice:** Sometimes service requires dedicated sacrifice, but the rewards are eternal. Queen Esther was willing to yield her life as a living sacrifice for the saving of her people. Romans 12:1 (AMP) "Therefore, I urge you, brothers and sisters, by the mercies of God, to present your bodies [dedicating all of yourselves, set apart] as a living sacrifice, holy and well-pleasing to God, *which is* your rational (logical, intelligent) act of worship."

Royal Reflection Questions:

1. How are you mastering the courage to survive, serve, and thrive?

2. How are you currently using your crown to serve others in your life, ministry, or business?

3. How can you increase the quality of your service?

4. How can you become more valuable?

5. In what areas do you need to shift your mindset from being served to serving others with grace and love?

6. Who are the people in your life that you are called to serve, and how can you support them more intentionally?

7. How can you lead by example in your home, business, or community, demonstrating God's love through your actions?

8. In what ways can you add more light, love, and service in our chaotic, fast-paced, technology-driven, competitive, and ever-evolving world?

9. If humility, service, and resilience are the embodiment of wisdom and leadership, then which characteristic do you need to enhance and strengthen?

10. What specific actions can you take to build a legacy of service that impacts future generations?

Queen, you were crowned to serve. Your royal authority is meant to uplift, empower, and pour out into others. As you step fully into this calling, remember that true greatness in the Kingdom of God is found in humble service. By serving others, you become the hands and feet of Christ, extending His love, mercy, and grace to a hurting world. May you rise in this divine calling, walking in the fullness of your royal service, leaving a legacy of transformation and love wherever you go. The most important work you will ever engage in is the opportunity to be of service to others.

Meditation Scripture

Psalm 84:11

"For the LORD God *is* a sun and shield; The LORD will give grace and glory; No good *thing* will He withhold from those who walk uprightly."

NOTE PAGE

Crowning Insights and Revelations

CHAPTER 7

Crowning for Legacy

"A good man leaves an inheritance to his children's children, but the sinner's wealth is laid up for the righteous."

– Proverbs 13:22 (ESV)

This concluding chapter is your commissioning into your royal role of purpose to influence and impact future generations, and to create a legacy in ways you've never imagined.

Your legacy is inevitably connected to God's purpose for your life. As you step into the fullness of your royal calling, your crown becomes a sacred accessory for a symbolic reminder of your royal inheritance.

The greatest queens are those who build something that outlives them, something that leaves an indelible mark on their families, communities, and the generations to come. Queens always sow seeds for the future. They understand that temporary delayed gratification is a means to creating and stewarding a future legacy that reflects the Kingdom of God, sustains significance, and creates generational wealth.

The Legacy of a Queen: Building for Generations

The legacy you leave is not simply about what you accumulate or achieve; it is about what you impart, what you build, and how you shape the destiny of those who come after you. As a Queen crowned for such a time as this, you are called to leave behind not just wealth, but a spiritual inheritance that will endure for generations.

As a Queen, you are entrusted with the power to shape destinies, influence lives, and build a foundation that will last long after you have transitioned.

You are responsible for preparing for the afterlife. Think about your death selflessly. Ask yourself: Whose life is going to be better because I was here? Will my life's work be a blessing and give my loved ones a competitive advantage of any kind? How you sow and spend your time, talents, steward your resources, invest and monetize your brilliance is going to make all the difference.

Your legacy is built and secured through wise estate and tax planning as well as your lifestyle. What you prioritize today will have ripple effects for the next generation. Your commitment to kingdom principles, spiritual growth and development, and servant leadership will echo through the generations as a testimony of God's faithfulness in your life.

Building your legacy is both Kingdom and financial as you are intentional about building a worthy inheritance. Your life is part of a great story, a divine narrative that transcends your individual journey and impacts future generations. Your legacy serves as a testament to the power of divine identity, purpose, discipline, and diligence.

Building Wealth and a Financial Legacy

First, let me say that I am not an attorney or a certified financial advisor. Please talk with your professional service providers about anything related to legal, financial, and estate affairs.

Here are some key questions for you to ponder on:

1. What does legacy mean to you?
2. What legacy milestones have you completed?
3. Have you developed a Legacy Vision Plan?
4. What does retirement mean for you? Have you considered long-term protection planning?
5. What will you have to accumulate in assets to be able to retire?
6. What are your short-term financial goals?
7. What are your long-term financial goals?
8. Have you given any thought to your business's exit plan?
9. Have you considered a tax liability assessment of your company?
10. How are you monetizing your intellectual property?

11. Do you have proper legal protection of your brilliance and brand?

12. What action steps do you need to take to live full out in the Vision and beyond?

Stay actively in pursuit of creating your Vision Legacy Plan and building legal protection along the journey.

Here are three basic pillars of wealth-building:

- Own your own business and teach your children how to start their own business early in life. Have conversations about economics and wealth-building. Once you start your own business, your financial outcomes will change. Ownership is more important than income.

- Stock market investment. Consistent stock market investment is one of the leading factors in determining who will be rich and who will not. Investors receive a large number of tax benefits.

- Real estate ownership. Being a homeowner gives you assets and growth in value, and tax benefits. Wealth comes from ownership.

Wealth-building is an ongoing, strategic, and power-moves journey across multiple generations. Protecting and preserving assets, building and nurturing covenant relationships, and creating a legacy include the following financial elements of preparation:

- **An estate plan** – a financial order of proper estate planning includes a will, trust, and power of attorney, living will, healthcare directives, financial power of attorney, and beneficiary designation.
- **A wealth plan** – a full financial picture including savings, retirement, investment accounts, and assets
- **Intellectual property protection plan** – patents, trademarks, copyright registrations, trade secrets, frameworks, methodologies, company name, your name, signature messages, training content,

curriculum, video content, podcasts, blogs, and articles

- **Investment portfolio plan** – Long-term and short-term investment strategy plans that build assets over time.

- **Insurance portfolio plan** – term life and whole life insurance, disability insurance, general liability insurance, professional liability insurance, health insurance, home insurance, car insurance, landlord insurance, and long-term care insurance.

- **Business succession plan** – a plan of your business future, financial goals, including a valuation of your company, and potential successors.

Your business is one of the primary keys to your financial legacy, and it has a bigger purpose than just making money. Plan wisely and sow the seeds that will take your success to the next level, even beyond your time on the throne.

Generational Influence: Shaping Futures

One of the most significant aspects of your legacy is the influence and impact you have on others. Whether in your family, your business, or your community, your influence can shape the future for generations to come. Above leaving financial wealth, legacy is about leaving wisdom, imparting knowledge, and instilling values that empower others to rise and roar.

Invest and guide your children to be CEOs, not just employees. Teach the values of family legacy, relationships, businesses, assets, and financial intelligence. Create a clear diamond vision and purpose for their lives beyond making enough money to pay bills.

Consider the leaders, mentors, and spiritual guides in your life. Their influence has shaped your story and journey. Now, as a Queen crowned for legacy, you are called to leave the same impact on the lives of others. Your ability to influence will determine the trajectory of those who follow in your footsteps, making your legacy one of transformation and elevation.

Kingdom Legacy: Stewarding Eternal Impact

Crowned for legacy is to build for now and create an eternal impact. As a Queen of Faith, your actions and decisions have eternal significance and great impact. What you build on this earth will carry on into the Kingdom of God, influencing generations that may never know you personally, but will benefit from the seeds you sow today.

A Kingdom legacy reflects the values of God's Kingdom, including core values, spiritual principles, relationships, justice, mercy, grace, faithfulness, stewardship, authority, hope, faith, and love. As a Queen, your role is to steward a legacy that reaches through eternity. This legacy will be seen in the lives you touch, the impact you make, and the generations you raise.

To create a lasting impact, be intentional in the choices and decisions you make. Align your heart with God's will and make decisions that will honor you as well as Him. A Queen crowned for legacy knows that her life is more than just her own; it is part of a greater divine plan that will have lasting effects long after she transitions to the Promised Land.

Ways to build a lasting legacy:

1. **Mentorship:** serve, invest in the next generation by pouring into others, sharing your knowledge and experiences, and guiding them to their own purpose. Strong families are one of the keys to a powerful legacy.

2. **Generosity:** give of your time, talents, and resources freely, knowing that what you sow today will reap an eternal harvest. (2 Corinthians 9:6-7)

3. **Faithfulness:** Be faithful in the small things, knowing that every act of obedience, kindness, and service will be honored and rewarded.

4. **Wisdom:** ask and pray for wisdom, live wisely, and make decisions that honor the God in you, knowing that your choices have eternal consequences.

Exodus 31:3

"I have filled him with the Spirit of God in wisdom

and skill, in understanding *and* intelligence, in knowledge, and in all kinds of craftsmanship."

Royal Reflections and Questions:

1. Start thinking about your business as the key to your financial legacy. How can you create income streams from the things that you own?
2. What kind of legacy do you want to have? How do you want to be remembered by future generations?
3. Get referrals for key professionals to support you, including an estate attorney, a small business attorney, an intellectual property attorney, and a certified financial planner.
4. How can you begin building a legacy of impact today, in your family, your community, or your business?
5. In what ways can you align your current actions with God's plan for an eternal legacy?
6. How are you using your crown to influence others and shape their destinies?

7. What action steps can you take to begin investing in others and building a lasting legacy? How can you empower loved ones to gain financial strength and security?

Queen, you were crowned not just for today, but for eternity. Your life is part of a divine story, a story that will continue to unfold through the generations you influence and the legacy you leave behind.

As you step into the fullness of your royal calling, remember that your crown is meant to create a legacy of purpose, impact, and transformation that will echo through time.

Take the time to craft your Vision Legacy Plan. May you build with wisdom and serve with grace. Leave a legacy that reflects the richness of your brilliance and the Kingdom of God in all its glory. Own your crown, live a prosperous, wealthy life.

Meditation Scripture

Proverbs 3:5-6

"Trust in *and* rely confidently on the LORD with all your heart and do not rely on your own insight *or* understanding. In all your ways know *and* acknowledge *and* recognize Him, And He will make your paths straight *and* smooth [removing obstacles that block your way]."

NOTE PAGE
Crowning Insights and Revelations

The Final Pour
The Oil. The Inner Excellence. The Flow.

Queen, if you're still reading this, I want you to know something sacred: this moment... this very sentence... is not the end. It is a divine New Beginning.

You have been crowned in oil, clothed in beauty, and called into greatness — not because of perfection, but because of divine purpose. Your crown was always waiting for you to say Yes, to rise in royal authority, and to cultivate the inner excellence that reflects the brilliance of the One who anointed you.

Please allow me to be transparent with you, at the beginning of this writing experience, I did not see this coming. I was not feeling it. Nevertheless, I moved forward out of obedience, but I didn't feel quite prepared. Truthfully, I didn't feel ready to *revisit* all the hard places, the pressing, the crushing, the rising, the refining. But the Holy Spirit whispered, *"This is not about your comfort—it's about My glory."* So, I surrendered with the release of faith and trust in God's Word... and, to my delightful surprise, the oil and words began to flow along with the refreshing tears of gratitude.

This book—*this Sacred Blueprint*—was birthed in the fire of personal purification, fresh revelation, healing, and undeniable transformational personal encounters with the Holy Spirit. I opened my heart and poured out my pain, and witnessed it become purpose. I released my tears and felt them transform into diamonds of destiny. I turned my vulnerability into victory and experienced my *resilience, reimagined* and a greater degree of inner excellence. And so can you.

You've walked through a *Divine Coronation* process unveiled through seven sacred chapters:

1. You were called in the **Crowning Act of a Queen**.
2. You unlocked sacred anointing and hidden flows in the **Crowning Oil Unlock**.
3. You were refined and rebuilt to shine in your inner excellence in the **Crowning Oil for a Resilient Queen**.

4. You gained wisdom, insight, strategy, and authority in the **Crowning Oil for Financial Authority**.

5. You stepped into courageous leadership in **Crowning to Reign**.

6. You discovered divine humility in **Crowning to Serve**.

7. And you were empowered to create wealth and build for future generations in **Crowning for Legacy**.

These chapters were not lessons, they were *prophetic portals of revealed truth, identity, healing, liberation, consecration, anointing, authority, and legacy*. Every revelation was a mirror of the greatness inside of you. Every page was a chamber. And every sentence was a stretch into the Queen you are becoming.

I pray this encounter with the Holy Spirit has ignited something within you. I pray you've cried, reflected, journaled, healed, and been re-awakened. I pray you feel empowered to *rest, reflect, and reign*, not from striving, but from alignment.

Queen… this is your Crowning Year. The Movement has begun—and yes, you're part of it. Your legacy is no longer a distant dream. Your pain is no longer just part of your past. Your story is your assignment. Your crown is your confirmation.

I want you to know that I'm here for you. Not just as an author… but as a midwife, a mentor, and a mantle-bearer. Together, we rise. Together, we reign. Together, we pour. Take up your oil. Lift your head high. AND GO… blaze trails, bless nations, and birth generational legacies.

You are the miracle, movement, and mantle.

With passion, compassion, and royal confidence in you,

Dr. Lougenia J. Rucker, Divine Diamonds Ministries

The Legacy Queens Manifesto

Crowned to Reign

The Legacy Queens Collective

An intimate movement of regal women destined to lead, love, and leave a legacy.

We are **Legacy Queens** anointed, appointed, aligned, and crowned for such a time as this. We are women of faith who wear our crowns not just as a hair adornment, but as divine assignments and an integral part of this Mantle Movement.

We stand united in our commitment to personal transformation, spiritual mastery, marketplace domination, and legacy building. Our mantle is sacred, our mission is clear, and our movement is unstoppable.

We don't compete — we commission.
We don't chase trends — we trailblaze truths.
We don't just age — we ascend in wisdom, grace, and multi-generational purpose.

We are the keepers of wisdom, the midwives of mantles, and the carriers of Kingdom blueprints for legacy living.

We are not afraid of time — we *redeem* it.
We don't shrink or settle with time — we expand in grace and influence.

Our years of service have refined us. Our scars have crowned us. Our voices are sacred, our presence is royal, and our leadership impact is eternal.

As part of the **Legacy Queens Collective**, we rise with:

- **Royal conviction** to lead with divine clarity and courage.
- **Prophetic grace** to love with open arms and fierce faith.
- **Sacred vision** to leave a path of impact that outlives us

We carry mantles that were prayed for, anointed, prophesied over, and preserved through every wilderness and spiritual war. Now, we release those mantles in power, purpose, and poised for the daughters, for the nations, and for the glory of God.

WE DECLARE:
We are *Crowned to Reign.*
We lead with heart.
We love with legacy.
We leave nothing buried that God called us to birth.

This is our movement. This is our mantle. This is our moment.

Together, we cultivate a circle of strength, sisterhood, and supernatural acceleration. In this Movement, we uplift, empower, and ignite the fire in one another. We hold space for expansion, for revelation, and for the undeniable manifestation of God's promises in our lives and businesses.

A Special Invitation to Legacy Queens:

This is your moment. Your divine appointment to step into a greater level of influence and impact. *The Legacy Queen Manifesto* is more than a declaration; it is a lifestyle, a commitment, and a transformation.

If you are ready to elevate to the next dimension, to own your mantle, and to walk boldly in your divine assignment, we invite you to join us. Become a part of a movement where power meets purpose, faith fuels action, and transformation is inevitable.

Visit https://**TrailblazingTransformations.com** to connect, engage, and take your rightful place in the Legacy Queen Movement.

Global Letter to the Nations

Arise, Shine, and Claim Your Kingdom Destiny

"Arise, shine, for your light has come; and the glory of the Lord has risen upon you."   – Isaiah 60:1

Beloved Nations:

As you read these words, know that a divine transformation movement is underway. One that carries the influence and power of heaven into every corner of the earth. We are called from the ashes of the past into the radiant light of a New Day. God has set in motion a transformation experience that not only redeems our souls but also propels us toward trailblazing Kingdom authority and eternal legacies.

In Isaiah 61, the Lord declares,
"He has sent me to bind up the brokenhearted, to proclaim liberty to captives, and release to prisoners; to proclaim the acceptable year of the Lord, and the day of vengeance of our God; to comfort all who mourn;"

These words remind us that every heartbroken soul, every captive spirit, and every shattered dream is destined for restoration. The divine anointing is breaking every chain, equipping us to shine as vessels of hope and agents of radical change.

Today, we declare that the wealth of transformation: spiritual, emotional, and financial, is our inheritance. We step into a legacy where resilience meets divine empowerment, and where every Queen is crowned with authority to lead, innovate, and create a future filled with peace and prosperity.

May you be empowered to arise higher, for the light of the Lord is upon you. May you carry the oil of anointing that refines, renews, and releases the fullness of your royal identity and destiny. May you join this prophetic Mantle Movement, not only to witness change but to be the CHANGE in your communities, nations, and the world.

Let this Global Letter serve as a rallying call for every heart that yearns for freedom, every mind that dares to dream, and every Queen that is ready to arise and be crowned with the beauty of transformation, the shine of personal brilliance, and the destiny of divine glory.

In His Eternal Love,

Dr. Lougenia J. Rucker
Marketplace Queen, Mentor, and Prophetic Trailblazer
Divine Diamonds Ministries, Apostle

A Global Commissioning Prayer

Dearest Queen, I rejoice with you as you have allowed yourself to be pushed out of your comfort zone. You have endured life and walked through the fire, refined like gold. You have suffered, pressed through the crushing, and now the oil of divine purpose flows freely upon you. You have been equipped, anointed, and crowned in excellence, not just for yourself but for the generations you are called to impact.

This is your **Moment of Ascension.** A time of a new life and a new way of living. The journey has been one of believing, shifting, breaking, decreeing, receiving, and rebuilding. But now, you stand fully awakened in your voice, story, and power. You are no longer confined by limitations or bound by past wounds, you are healed, free, elevated, unapologetic, and unstoppable.

- You shall understand and embrace your innate gifts, talents, inner excellence, and what you are uniquely gifted to do. Dreams shall become reality.

- You shall walk with clarity, humility, and unwavering faith.
- You shall govern your life and kingdom assignments with wisdom, servant leadership, and divine strategy.
- You shall serve, build, bless, and break barriers with courage and conviction.
- You shall collaborate and support the development of a community that appreciates the building of generational wealth and financial legacies.
- You shall confidently reign in credibility, influence, impact, and abundance on purpose to empower and elevate the next generation of Queens.

Commissioning Charge: Arise, Shine and Take Your Royal Position and Reign...

- ❖ Your name is written in the heavens as a Queen of Faith and Excellence; therefore, continue to call forth the strength to surge forward.
- ❖ Your legacy unfolds as you step beyond your comfort zone with a fresh anointing, renewed self-mastery, and a relentless boldness to fulfill your calling, assignment, and destiny.

- ❖ Your anointing will break generational chains and curses as rivers of living water flow, adding great value, and everything you touch will prosper.
- ❖ Your throne is established in divine excellence, resilience, integrity, and authority.

You are not just stepping forward, you are ASCENDING. Remain encouraged, prayerful, hopeful, and grateful. Pray in your secret place and anoint yourself daily. The world will witness your grace and excellence, and the Heavens will rejoice in your reign. The oil and the holy seal of God are upon your life.

Sustain momentum by joining the *Crowned to Reign* Movement. Keep evolving, stay focused, and stay the course. Do not be discouraged, do not waver, because the work you are doing is most important. The new creative anointing is springing forward, and there shall be a manifestation of it for generations to come. Arise, and look to the Future.

In Jesus' name. AMEN.

Divine Diamonds Ministries

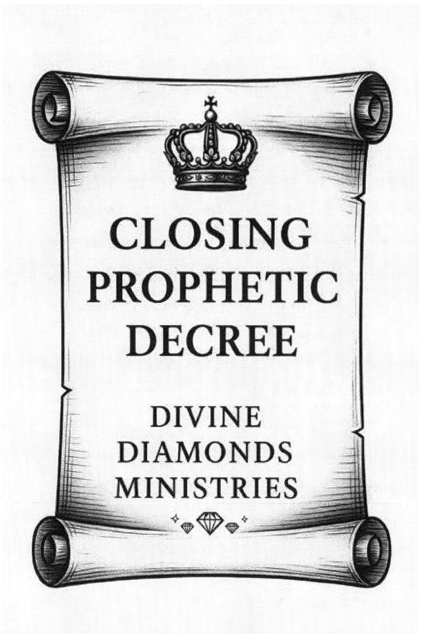

CLOSING
PROPHETIC
DECREE

DIVINE
DIAMONDS
MINISTRIES

Closing Prophetic Decree

"The Queen's Final Decree: Anointed to Reign, Commissioned to Shine"

I Decree that I am no longer waiting for permission — Heaven has already crowned me:

I arise from the ashes of every past season, anointed with fresh oil, clothed in royal garments, and filled with divine passion, wisdom, grace, resilience, and excellence.

I walk in clarity, confidence, and courage.

I command my soul to align with God's timing, trust in His truth, rejoice in His joy, and release the weight of fear, guilt, shame, rejection, and unworthiness.

I Decree that I am crowned for such a time as this:

My mind is sound and clear. My temple is strong, healthy, and resilient. My voice carries prophetic insight and instructions. My words bring understanding, healing, and breakthrough.

My hands create wealth and build a legacy.

My steps are ordered by the Lord, and I walk in divine alignment and authority.

I Decree that I am commissioned to reign:

To rise as a light in dark places.

To lead with compassion and conviction.

To bless generations with the oil of wisdom and mentorship. To speak life, unlock vision, and build with a passionate fire.

I am crowned not for vanity, but for victory.

Not for performance, but for purpose.

Not for applause, but for assignment.

I am not what I've been through. I am who God says I am.

From this moment forward, I live, lead, and love from the throne of grace He designed for me.

I am a Queen crowned and anointed to reign, born to thrive and sent to shine in my brilliance.

And I shall not be moved out of my position, in Jesus' name.

"Arise, shine, for your light has come, and the glory of the Lord rises upon you." — *Isaiah 60:1*

Divine Diamonds Ministries Collective

Recommended Reading List

- ***The 10 Commandments of the Wealth Transfer*** by Dr. Lougenia J. Rucker
- ***5 Power Moves of the Wealth Transfer*** by Dr. Lougenia J. Rucker
- ***Game-Changer: Why Not You*** by Dr. Lougenia J. Rucker
- ***When God Speaks*** by Joshua Giles
- ***Move to Millions*** by Dr. Darnyelle Jervey Harmon
- ***The Wealth Choice*** by Dennis Kimbro
- ***Identity*** by Dr. Stephanie M. Kirkland
- ***Resilience @ Work*** by Simon T. Bailey
- ***Napoleon Hill's Your Millionaire Mindset*** by Don Green, The Napoleon Hill Foundation
- ***10 Commandments of Black Economic Power*** by Dr. Boyce Watkins
- ***Sacred Rest*** by Saundra Dalton-Smith, MD
- ***Commanding Your Money*** by Dwann Homes | Rosemary Winbush

Resources

https://www.wealthcomesnow.com

https://www.trailblazingtransformations.com

Diamond Heart Prophetic Business Mentorship™

One-to-One Prophetic Mentorship for Kingdom Clarity and Confidence

Step into a sacred space of prophetic alignment where your heart is refined like a diamond. The *Diamond Heart Prophetic Mentorship* is a transformational one-to-one mentorship experience designed to awaken your clarity, activate bold confidence, and empower you with the courage to take your next God-ordained step within your genius zone. If you're ready for divine direction, strategic guidance, and compassionate accountability, this is your moment to rise and reign.

The Ultimate Game-Changer Wealth-Building Network & Mastermind™

Your 12-Month Prophetic Hub for Wealth Strategy, Building, and Expansion

This is more than a network—it's a divine movement of wealth builders, trailblazers, and prophetic visionaries. The *Ultimate Game-Changer Wealth-Building Prophetic Network & Mastermind* is your monthly gathering place for kingdom collaboration, mastermind brilliance, and spiritual downloads that align your wealth vision with heaven's strategy. Engage in power-packed strategy sessions and prophetic insight that sharpen your next move in the marketplace.

Game-Changer Coaching Program™

An 8-Week Activation into Your Boldest, Bravest Self

Using the signature 5-Cs Game-Changer Framework™—**Commitment, Clarity, Confidence, Courage, and Community/Call to Action**—this dynamic 8-week group coaching program will stretch you, sharpen you, and support you in unlocking new levels of purpose and impact. Designed for faith-driven visionaries ready to break barriers and walk in unstoppable momentum, this program is your divine invitation to show up, speak up, and power up like the Game-Changer you are!

Want to be a Coach? Learn more about the Game-Changer Coaching Certification Program.

NEW Certification Program
Crowned to Reign™

A Queen's Certification in Leadership, Legacy & Kingdom Impact

***Crowned to Reign*™ is a groundbreaking certification and training program inspired by the transformational message of *A Queen's Crown*.**

Are you ready to walk boldly in your divine assignment and equip others to do the same? This elite program equips you with spiritual, prophetic, and leadership tools to embody and teach the principles of royalty, resilience, and reign. Learn how to build your legacy, serve with divine authority, and lead others in activating their crowning call. This is for the Queen, ready to multiply her impact, extend her mantle, and serve as a certified Kingdom Influencer.

Please Take a Moment to Pass the Blessing Forward

"People who help others (with zero expectations) experience higher levels of fulfillment, live longer, and make more money."   — Alex Hormozi

Queen, if this book has blessed you in any way—if even one page ignited your faith, stirred your purpose, or helped you see your crown more clearly, I humbly invite you to pass the blessing forward.

Write a Review on Amazon:

Your words have power. Leaving a thoughtful review not only supports the message of *A Queen's Crown* but also helps this sacred blueprint reach other women who are waiting to rise into their royal identity. Your voice matters!

Subscribe to My YouTube Channel:
https://www.youtube.com/@DivineDiamondsIntl

Be the first to receive more prophetic teachings, empowering declarations, behind-the-scenes mentorship moments, and inspiration to fuel your reign. This is your invitation to stay connected and continue growing in community and divine purpose.

Thank you in advance for your love, support, and willingness to shine the brilliance forward. Together, we build the movement, one Queen at a time.

Acknowledgments

To the God in me, the Holy One who knew me before I was formed in my mother's womb — I honor You. Thank you for breathing life into every word and guiding my heart through every chapter. Thank you, Holy Spirit, for being my Divine Midwife, scribe, teacher, comforter, and activator. You whispered a vision in the dark and brought light to the path. I could not have poured this oil without Your presence.

To my Trailblazing Publishing Team, thank you for being the wind beneath my wings and helping me steward this vision with excellence. Your creative brilliance, spirit-led guidance, and unwavering support helped me give birth to not just a book, but a Movement.

To my Divine Diamonds Ministries: Game-Changer Coaching Clients™ and my beloved Diamond Heart Mentees, you are a living testament to resilience, courage, and Kingdom brilliance. Thank you for trusting me to walk with you, guide you, and pour into your journey. You inspire me every day to go deeper, reach higher, and continue to serve with authenticity and power.

This book was written with you in mind. Your journey matters. Your story matters. Your crown matters. Together, we rise and reign.

Bonus Gift

A Queen's Prophetic Crown of Glory

Receive Your Free Gift: *"A Queen's Prophetic Crown of Glory"*

This powerful decree was designed to anchor your divine identity and inner excellence. It will support you to reign with clarity, courage, and conviction. Download it, print it, and declare it daily as a royal affirmation of the Queen you are.

Visit: https://trailblazingtransformations.com/QueensGift to receive your **FREE Prophetic Download.**

Let this be your daily declaration and your next step into the Queen's Crown to Reign Movement.

The Lasting Word
Your Crown Awaits

Queen, you have journeyed through the sacred unveiling of this prophetic blueprint. From ashes to beauty, from anointing to reign, from purpose to prophetic legacy, you have been refined by fire, anointed by the oil of the Holy Spirit, and elevated to embody inner excellence and greatness.

You are not who you once were. You have been prepared for impact, crowned for destiny, and ignited to reign with power, purity, and purpose. Now, you are commissioned to ascend into your next dimension, a realm where royal identity, inner excellence, divine authority, and generational legacy converge. This is your call to reign higher, shine brighter, lead bolder, and walk fully in the unstoppable power of your Queen's Crown. Your next dimension awaits.

This was never just about a book; it was about Becoming. You've read chapters anointed with revelation, poured in oil, and ignited with divine fire. Each one carved out space for transformation, breaking out new clarity, courage, and commitment within you. You've unlocked the crowning oil, embraced your identity, and stepped into prophetic authority. Now, it is time to rise and reign.

Let these last words echo in your spirit: You are not invisible. You are invincible. You are not just a woman—you are a royal vessel. A Queen, crowned not by culture, but by the King of Kings.

Your crown is not a decoration; it is a declaration. It declares that you have overcome. It declares that you are worthy. It declares that you are anointed to lead, love, build, bless, and blaze new trails.

This book was born from my crushing, through divine whispers in the midnight hour, sacred oil flowing from hidden places, and healing tears that poured as I wrote. It is a piece of my soul, a part of my legacy. A gift to women like you who are being called to rise higher. Know that as I poured out, I was healed too.

This is the year of your Crowning Moment, your invitation to rest, reflect, reposition and reign. I pray you are healed, renewed, and feel worthy of the Call. And above all, I pray you embrace the divine mantle that now rests upon your life.

Step into the reign of your divine empowerment. Let your legacy roar for the glory of God.

With Royal Love and Kingdom Oil,

Dr. Lougenia J. Rucker

Meet The Trailblazer Author

The Queen Behind the Movement

Dr. Lougenia J. Rucker is more than a transformational speaker and published author from Philadelphia, PA. She is a *divine trailblazing force of transformation and has an apostolic/prophetic* voice, a visionary book coach, a 4x Best Seller Author, a mentor, and a spiritual strategist to Kingdom Queens worldwide. With a radiant blend of authenticity, compassion, resilience, and spiritual fire, she walks boldly in her God-ordained assignment to coach, crown, and commission women into their next-level calling in their genius zone.

Forged from pain into purpose, her journey from *tragedy to trailblazer* has inspired thousands to rise from their ashes and embrace a life of clarity, confidence, and courageous dominion. A life-altering hit-and-run accident, seasons of caregiving, abandonment, and burnout, the heartbreak of divorce, and the triumph of healing and restoration have all become sacred oil poured out on every page she writes and every life she touches.

For almost a decade, she has coached, anointed, and crowned women through her Game-Changer Coaching Program, empowering them to unlock their brilliance, embrace the authority of their divine identity, and build generational legacy.

Her voice is a vessel of empowerment, *love, and illumination*, her message a clarion call to change and reign, and her life a living testimony that *resilience reimagined* is possible for every woman who dares to believe again.

As the Founding Apostle of Divine Diamonds Ministries in 2009, she is committed to empowering women to live their best lives *on purpose*, with vision, and unapologetically in their royal zone of healing, fulfillment, and prosperity.

Because of her surrender, the anointing of God flows through her books, programs, services, prophetic teachings, and one-on-one mentorship. Dr. Rucker is leaving a legacy of empowered Queens who arise in beauty, serve in humility, lead with wisdom, and reign with glory and prosperity.

Contact Dr. Lougenia J. Rucker:

Book Dr. Rucker to Speak at Your Event:
Email: DrLougenia@trailblazingtransformations.com |
(484)-443-3889
https://www.trailblazingtransformations.com

Connect with Dr. Lougenia J. Rucker

Divine Diamonds Ministries -

https://www.divinediamondsministries.ning.com

LinkedIn -

https://www.linkedin.com/in/lougeniatrailblazer

Youtube -

https://www.youtube.com/@DivineDiamondsIntl

Facebook -

https://www.Facebook/LougeniaJRucker